WHAT REALLY MATTERS

Stories That Invite Going Slowly and Taking Time

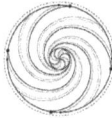

Keith Kron

Edited by Barbara Child

Island Shore
P R E S S

Island Shore Press™
PROVIDENCE, RI 02909

10 9 8 7 6 5 4 3 2

First Edition 2021
Printed in the United States of America

ISBN: 978-0-578-88709-8
Library of Congress Control Number: 2021906478

Cover & book design by CenterPointe Media
www.CenterPointeMedia.com

Dedicated to the Memory of
Cynthia L. Prescott

January 2, 1951—May 29, 2016

Thank you for being my colleague, friend,
comic relief, and thought partner.
Thank you for going slowly with me.
I know I am not alone in missing you.
I carry you with me each day.
We had so little time.

"We must go slowly. We have so little time."
—RON CHISOLM, BLACK ELDER,
TEACHING THE WORK OF ENDING RACISM

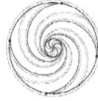

Contents

What Really Matters

Introduction

"You should write a book!" For years people have been saying this to Keith Kron in comments on his social media posts about his encounters, mostly by chance, with people in such places as airports, check-out lines in stores, and restaurants. It always pleases me to see these comments. After all, he and I have been good friends for over a quarter century, and I love to see his inquisitive, caring, and insightful nature recognized and applauded by others. Yes, and his humor and incisiveness as well. When Keith Kron says something, especially publicly, you can count on its being worth paying attention to.

Keith and I met as seminary students in Berkeley, California, both of us coming to ministry after thriving for years in other professions. He had been an elementary school teacher, and I learned in time of his huge personal library, including a remarkable collection of children's books. During our frequent after-class dinners, I learned lots of other things too. For example, Keith loves to play tennis, and he teaches tennis as well. He is a diabetic, and if he kept all the sweetener packets he has emptied over the years, they might number as many as his books.

Such facts about my friend Keith might seem incidental, but they also sometimes turn out to be significant in the saga of his travels. His travels are many, just about constant, at least until the 2020 pandemic changed his working life. After we both graduated from seminary in 1996, while I went off to serve one congregation after another as an interim minister, Keith has ministered in the world of denominational administration for the Unitarian Universalist Association. For the last decade, he has been serving as the Director of Ministerial Transitions, shepherding ministers through the complicated process of transition from one church to the next and shepherding congregations through the equally complicated process of transition from one minister to the next. I have long ago lost count of the many hundreds of congregations Keith has visited, the number of anti-oppression trainings he has facilitated, and the thorny paths he has helped both ministers and congregational leaders negotiate. As far as I can tell, he is just about universally loved, not just respected, by Unitarian Universalists across the land.

And then there are all those other people that Keith, the inveterate people person, has engaged with at a tennis match, on some airplane or train, or in some restaurant or store. Knowing him as I do, even though I haven't been present for all those encounters, I have loved every word he has written about them on social media. And so after I had read over and over again comments on his posts saying, "You ought to write a book," I began to say to myself, "You already have. It's already there, in those years of posts on social media."

The next step was a natural. Keith and I had loved working together before as co-editors of *In the Interim*, a collection of essays on interim ministry written by colleagues of ours and published by Skinner House Books, the Unitarian Universalist Association's in-house publisher. In essence, what happened next was that I said to him, "Let's do this," and he said, "Yes, let's." And *voila,* here you are, with this collection of his stories! May you discover in it as much thoughtful reflection and joy in living as it brought to Keith and me as we wove them together to make this book.

—Barbara Child

What Really Matters

Praise for *What Really Matters*

What Really Matters offers readers a collection of vignettes that taken together form an everyday living prayer that we might treat each other with decency and respect. With humor and kindness, *What Really Matters* serves as a window into the moments of connection in human living that make us more whole.

—Rev. Dr. Sofia Betancourt, Associate Professor of
Unitarian Universalist Theologies and Ethics,
Starr King School for the Ministry

I loved *What Really Matters*. Those of us who are called to search for meaning in our lives and to share it—we call ourselves ministers and teachers and parents and friends—will recognize ourselves in this book. I was reminded again and again that we are not called to have all the answers, we are called to be present to our lives. This book reminds us that we live life moment to moment and day by day. Keith Kron also reminds us that grace can be discovered in the midst of the real lives we live. The reminder is grace too.

—Rev. Bill Sinkford, Former President,
Unitarian Universalist Association

If you don't know a sweet, witty, observant person, you will after reading Keith Kron's collection of stories. He shops for groceries, plays avid tennis, travels (and over-packs) for work, and collects children's books, thereby creating a life of wry joy and kindness, even in airports. About books he says, "I love books. They tell stories of value that are not about my life, but in some ways become a part of my life and story—at least enriching it." Well, Keith Kron's stories are now a welcome part of my life and hopefully will be in yours.

—Rev. Jane Ranney Rzepka, author of *A Small Heaven: A Meditation Manual*; *From Zip Lines to Hosaphones: Dispatches from the Search for Truth and Meaning*; and *Thematic Preaching*

Lost keys, long grocery lines, delayed airplanes cause many of us to feel as if we are alone in a hostile universe. Keith Kron has made the radical decision to use precisely these moments for connection and humanity. In this book, he shares those moments with us, and in so doing makes us all a bit more human.

—Rev. Meg Riley, co-Moderator, Unitarian Universalist Association; editor of *Testimony: The Transformative Power of Unitarian Universalism* and *Shelter in This Place: Meditations on 2020*

In these brutal times, reading Keith Kron's book *What Really Matters* has been a welcome balm, reminding us of the care—and self-care—human beings need to give and to receive. I plan to keep it on my nightstand, to dip into on the hard days, just to be reminded of grace.

—Rev. Rosemary Bray McNatt, President, Starr King School for the Ministry; author of *Unafraid of the Dark*

Preface

Every year I average one or two calls or emails about a minister who has died unexpectedly while serving a congregation. So I was not surprised by the email informing me that one of our ministers in the South had died. Chances were I would discover that the minister was someone I knew and I would remember a personal story that would help me begin planning how to help the congregation and the minister's family get ready for what would happen next. But then I learned an hour later that the minister who had died was my seminary classmate and good friend Cynthia.

Whom I'd known for 22 years. With whom I had a daily email exchange. Whose mother's memorial service I'd led. Who apparently had sent me the last email she ever wrote before suffering a heart attack and dying on Friday night alone, though her two housemates, her cats Jack and Elvis, were there, now with only each other to entertain.

I thought of Jack and Elvis and wondered where they might go to live now. I remembered how excited Cynthia was when she got them. We had this exchange in a series of emails:

Cynthia wrote to me, "I'm going to get a cat, maybe two, today. It's time to replace Isabel (her previous cat who'd died a year before)."

I wrote back, "Get ones that will truly be entertaining. Maybe one that does Jack Benny impressions or sings like Bette Midler."

To which Cynthia replied, "I want cats that can juggle pit bulls."

"Who doesn't?" I responded.

And now Jack and Elvis were alone. I wondered if they'd feel the loss.

It took me a few weeks to realize I was alone. There would be no one to replace Cynthia in my life. It took longer for me to begin to grapple with the impact that had on me.

When I met Cynthia in seminary, she had moved from Maine to California for a new life. Someone had worried that she might be an angry person, but mostly to me she seemed grateful and relieved to have the opportunity to be pursuing life on her own terms, reveling in a new world with new possibilities. Because we lived in the same dormitory, we shared common meals and spaces together—as well as some classes. She'd come as a former congregational president, and I had spent seven years on my home congregation's board. We liked the same things about congregational life. But we also shared laughter—finding commonality in not taking things too seriously and finding humor in both big and little things. And the humor was often directed at each other, becoming a common language as well as a lens through which to see the world.

After seminary, separated by geographical distance, we began the ritual of daily email exchanges. These were observations on what was going on around us as well as what was happening to us, and what, almost always with humor, we felt about it all. Our email messages were something to look forward to and we both did—for more than two decades.

And then one Saturday in May she didn't respond. It wasn't that unusual. Saturday was often sermon writing day for her. It wasn't out of the ordinary for one of us to miss an occasional day. We usually made up for it with two (or six) messages the next day. I didn't think much of it.

But then that Sunday afternoon, when she had failed to show up at church, a church member went over to check on her. And eventually found her. Word spread quickly. And soon I had two phone calls.

It wasn't just work. It was personal. Very personal.

Days passed, and I began to be aware that my inbox was heavier and not lighter. Heavier at least partly because while I was used to my daily release of stories and observations, I was now holding them in—and holding on to them. I trudged on, because that's what you do. Your life goes on even when a part of it leaves you. Or rather that part of your life reconfigures itself into memory and echo, and you find yourself looking mostly backwards.

Grief isn't a moment. It's a companion you learn to live with. Now I had to learn to live with my new companion. Thomas Moore once wrote something like this: "A friendship may not have to endure throughout life in order to leave its eternal mark on the soul." My soul was host to many companions so I knew what I was in for. I was well practiced. Yet this would be hard.

My Appalachian family is highly empathic, very aware of the feelings of those around us. Often we can figure out what is going on in someone's life without their saying anything. Whatever combination of genetics and culture is in play means less than knowing we are on each other's minds a lot. It also leads us to less direct communication.

As my folks neared 80, they were quite intentional about making sure I didn't worry about them, another family trait. I'd helped them figure out social media enough so they could follow me and be connected with other family as they got older. Since they had said they wanted to know how I was doing more than they wanted to tell me how they were doing, I began posting on social media a daily sentence or two, often about playing tennis though occasionally about something funny, just to let them know I was doing fine and they didn't need to worry. After all, they had taught me well. And maybe, while I was at it, I thought I might have a chance now and then to expand their world a little bit.

Cynthia often commented in her emails about my posts on social media, which often sparked a longer exchange between us. Over time, I realized I was using my posts also to write to Cynthia, that the daily emails had shifted to become daily posts on social media, and then the postings slowly became more expansive and more open. It didn't hurt of course that other people seemed to like them too. What had started as a nightly note to my parents had evolved. I found myself writing with Cynthia whispering over my shoulder or more likely just silently smirking, yet I knew she was there.

My evolving realization is that when Cynthia died, I stopped marveling, stopped noticing, and stopped being fully in the world. And as some of the memories and echoes began to feel further away (which I also was mourning), others were telling me to keep marveling, keep noticing, find the pleasure that was still out there.

Being present to yourself, to the person in front of you, and to the world around you is hard when you have so many companions inside you. Grief tempts you to look back and have it be your only companion. But eventually you do notice that the world is moving, and then you begin to make efforts to move with it, often with great resistance and not at the same pace. Perhaps that's one of grief's important lessons: move at your own pace.

It was writing to Cynthia again on social media that connected me and allowed me to relearn how to be with those around me. Whether it was at the grocery store, on the train, or somewhere else, the observations and stories I wrote and shared on social media were replenishing and life-affirming for me. I could laugh again with people, at people, at myself. Laughter again became one of my companions. It wasn't that I missed Cynthia less. I just found the place for her in my soul that was more than grief. I discovered that life is about being present to more than one feeling at the same time, even when feelings contradict each other.

The stories that follow are my attempts to relearn how to be present to the world, to others, and to myself. These stories are not about grief, but they are in part about living with grief. If they don't feel like grief stories, then perhaps I've succeeded.

The expressed wishes from others that I collect some of my social media posts and put them into a book filled me at first with a general indifference. At first I reluctantly agreed, as long as someone else would do the work of gathering them. It was flattering and I felt a bit glib. It was only when I talked with my friend Barbara about a possible collection and began to talk with her about why I had written my stories that all the feelings about them became present and real. I thank her and others for stubborn encouragement. They all helped make this happen. My greatest hope is that my stories will help you be present to your stories. Then I hope you will share them. You won't be alone.

—Keith Kron

What Really Matters

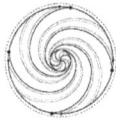

More Human
than Otherwise

What Really Matters

"Sir!?" I had just entered the grocery store a few minutes before closing, and when I turned around, there was a young African American man rushing toward me, holding something. "Are these your keys?"

They were. "Thank you," I said.

"No problem, sir. They were in front of the door. They must have fallen out of your pocket when you hurried in."

When would I have noticed? I had been trying to get out of the cold, too stubborn to put my gloves on and regretting it.

"Let me give you something," I stammered, realizing what it would feel like if my home and car keys were lost.

He smiled and shook his head. "It's nothing. Anyone would have done this." He dashed off before I could say, "No, they wouldn't." I was left standing there, grateful for this thoughtful teenager, who made my night a lot less anxious than it might have become. I won't forget his smile either as he handed me my keys before leaving. In an age of incivility, little acts like this young man's go a long way.

I have no idea what the woman in the car behind me was singing along with when I pulled out of the commuter rail parking lot this afternoon, but she was singing with such gusto I couldn't help wanting to sing along with her.

Then she noticed I was watching in my rearview mirror. It startled her and she stopped singing, looking embarrassed.

That made me sad, so I gave her a thumbs up.

She smiled and resumed singing.

I left the parking lot wishing everyone could have a little of the joy she was clearly having.

I recommend random hugs.

In the grocery store tonight after tennis, someone left a cell phone in the lane, clearly setting it down when they were bagging their groceries. I saw it when I bagged mine and turned it in. The couple who'd been in front of me were putting their last bag of groceries in their truck when I went out. I asked them if they had left a phone in the store.

The man slapped his pocket. "I must have."

"It's in the store," I said. "I gave it to one of the employees."

He started to run to the store, stopped, and ran back to me. "Thank you," he said and gave me a bear hug.

His girlfriend just beamed at us. It kind of made my night.

I was supposed to have the night off from tennis, but I subbed in, and it was fun.

But when I left the tennis club, I saw that my gas gauge was on empty. I checked the odometer as I pulled into the gas station—zero miles left.

I went for my credit card. No credit card, because there was no wallet. Search brought no luck. It had to be back at the tennis club.

But I needed gas, so I scrounged around in the car and found a dollar in change. Which should have been enough.

But as I told the cashier what had happened, he took all the pennies out of the little change holder and said, "Let's make it $1.14."

I accepted that and pumped $1.14 worth.

Later I found my wallet in the trunk of my car where it had fallen when I was putting in my tennis bag in.

A huge shout-out to the gas station cashier, who went beyond what he needed to do to help.

⟳

I'm guessing the woman with long tassels on her boots—the one who probably tripped on a tassel, which is what caused her nearly to fall alongside me as we raced to catch the train, the one who then waved me on when I stopped to help her, the one who actually said, "You go on without me," and then when I looked at her, said more earnestly, "You go, and save yourself"—has had a flair for the dramatic all of her life.

I have discovered that being diabetic does come with some gifts. After my diagnosis, I began taking care of my needs better than I had before.

For instance, in between teaching tennis and playing tennis, I had a dinner break. When I went to the nearby grocery store to get dinner at their good salad bar, I arrived just as the grocer was wheeling it away. I told him why I ate there on Wednesday nights, and he literally rolled the entire salad bar back out just for me.

I would never have had that conversation before my diagnosis. And I could tell he felt good about accommodating me.

On the plane to Oklahoma City from Baltimore, an older man sat next to me. He spoke very little English but enough to get by. He was headed to Dallas and was afraid he had gotten on the wrong plane. I asked to see his ticket, and fortunately he was just to change planes in Oklahoma City. I tried to explain that to him, and he seemed to get it. Mostly he slept. But when we touched down, he seemed nervous again.

Given that this was Oklahoma City and no airline's hub, I assumed there were only at most two more gates for the same airline. He wanted to get off right away, and it took him a moment to realize there was an order (such as it is) to getting off an airplane.

I motioned to him to follow me as we got off, and sure enough the gate for Dallas was next door. I told him this was his gate and wished him good luck. He stuck out his hand and we shook. And then he surprised me by hugging me.

On this airline it didn't seem likely that he was an international traveler. He had sat with a tied plastic bag in his lap during the entire three-hour flight from Baltimore to Oklahoma City. I wished I knew his story. Was this his first flight? Ever? Where was he from and where was he going? Why don't I know Spanish? (Not that three years of high school French have done me much good over the years.)

I hugged him back and waved good-bye, disappointed that I hadn't engaged him more, and impressed that something so little as helping him get to his next flight had made an impact.

Later, when I went to get my rental car, I discovered I had not reserved it for the right time, but for six hours earlier. I waited in line and explained what I had done. The agent smiled. "Thank you for being so nice about it," she said.

I nearly gasped. "It was my fault. I typed in the wrong number."

"Most people aren't so nice," she said with emphasis.

Later, in the grocery store getting supplies and snacks, I passed four younger guys, probably early 20's, though as I get older, my guesses about age are often way off. These white guys were clearly having a good time, oblivious of the older African American gentleman they nearly ran into, and I noticed that nearly every other one of their words was a curse word punctuating their laughter.

This evening's encounters got me thinking about manners. First, I hope that a very kind man who doesn't speak English very fluently made it to Dallas (or wherever was his actual destination). I also wish we could always take responsibility when we mess up and not expect others to have prevented it. And finally, I would like us always to notice when there are others around, maybe trying to make it through the grocery store and through life itself without being run over, unseen, and not respected.

A little tennis, even when you don't play well, is good for the soul. Why? one might ask.

The answer is that I spent 90 minutes cursing a tennis player instead of thinking about work. Therapy comes in many forms.

Sign of the apocalypse in Massachusetts: I go into a Super Store. I find everything I'm looking for—no, that's not the sign—including all the groceries for my crock pot meal of beef and vegetables.

The woman checking me out gets through most of my items and then holds up a bag of carrots. "These don't look as good as your other bag. I'll put these aside while you go get a better one."

There are two people in line behind me. Upon hearing this, they both actually smile. One even nods her head vigorously. "Just walk," the nodder says just before I break into a sprint. Groceries are on the other side of the store. "We'll wait," she adds, smiling more broadly.

Did I not leave Ohio? I ask myself. Did I get transported to Tennessee and not know it? Is this a dream? Are the three people at the check-out all zombies?

Apparently, the answer to all these questions is no. When I return, the cashier smiles, actually looks at my new bag of carrots, and says, "These are much better. You eat very healthy."

I pay for my food with my debit card with a chip, which means it takes longer than swiping. "I hate the new chip," I say. "It takes so much longer than before."

"I know." The cashier nods pleasantly. "But apparently it's safer, and I bet the speed will improve. Your veggies are in two bags. The meats are in another. And the rest is in three other bags, depending on whether it's food, household, or toiletries. I didn't bag the oranges since they were already in a bag. I hope that's okay."

Who is this woman? And does she mop and do windows? "It's fine. Thank you."

"You're welcome." She beams, handing me my receipt. "Have a good evening."

"You too," I stammer, still stunned since I've never seen this behavior in Massachusetts before. Ever. Must be global warming, right?

I went into the grocery store after a really nice barbecue dinner with a colleague. I decided to keep listening to music on my iPod as I went through the store. Sure enough, when I stopped to browse at the shoelaces, I found myself swaying to the music of Maroon 5 and Kendrick Lamar.

At first I didn't notice the interracial couple strolling up the aisle. But they noticed me. The African American man smirked slightly and then told the white woman he was with (borrowing one of my all-time favorite movie lines), "I'll have what he's having."

The woman looked at me. "What are you listening to?"

"'Don't Wanna Know' by Maroon 5 and Kendrick Lamar." I smiled sheepishly.

"I'd be dancing too," she said. She smiled and nodded, and they walked on past me.

But when they had walked past and looked back, I took their smiles as a cue and started dancing again. It kind of made my night.

There's a woman on the commuter train who always comes into the car with her bulldog. He's a happy fellow who loves to have his ears scratched by the conductor. I'm not sure who enjoys it more.

Today the bulldog stood on the edge of the armrest of the three-person seat across the aisle from me, hopped down, and came over for a visit. He proceeded to lick me profusely and cuddle, which I found amusing.

The owner called him back as the train slowed at the next stop. Reluctantly he left me and returned to her.

A new passenger sat down next to me in the two-person seat, where we were somewhat crammed together. The woman and the dog still had the three-person seat to themselves.

The dog looked at the new guy and, I swear, gave him a jealous look.

The guy didn't even look at the dog but eyed his phone.

The dog looked at me and then went and snuggled with his owner.

I proceeded to give the dog a jealous look. It seemed only fair.

Today I got a phone call from my old tennis club. A woman had found keys on the commuter rail with my old membership tag attached. The woman called the club, and they called me and gave me the woman's name and phone number. Her name was Valerie. I called her, and we agreed on a time and place to meet.

I thanked her and tried to give her some money, letting her know that she had saved me about $200. But she refused, even though she had gone out of her way to get my keys to me. She said she cleans the trains and found them.

Here's to Valerie for going the extra mile for another person. May the rest of us live up to her standards.

Today was all about spring cleaning. It was so nice to have a day off. I was finally going to rearrange the bedroom to include the new dresser. This involved moving the old dresser. This involved moving the cables and wires for the bedroom TV, cable box, and DVD player. This involved accidentally knocking the cable box off a dresser. This involved the TV and DVD player following the lead of the cable box. This involved cracking the TV screen. Sigh.

Fortunately, there's a deep discount store with a Memorial Day Sale, which meant I splurged on a TV—and got one seven inches larger than the previous one, at the same price. It's now installed and the wires are tucked away. The dressers are in their right places. My cleaning even produced six loads of trash.

Today's theological question: Why does one keep old, frayed auxiliary cords that long ago stopped working?

Mostly I putzed today. I'd forgotten how much I enjoy putzing. Maybe spring cleaning is after all about more than cleaning. It's about reflecting, reassessing, and changing speeds. Maybe I need more days like this one.

I was on my way home after a great week and a half of holidays. I pulled up to my hotel in the middle of nowhere—so nowhere that when the road in front of the hotel ended in a T, I nearly drove into a pond as there was no stop sign and no nearby light.

When I went up to the front desk in the hotel, I was all set to check in. I handed my license and card to the clerk. She looked at both for a second before it dawned on her. "You're checking in?" She finally recovered.

"Yes."

"What's your name?"

I had handed her my license, but oh well. "Kron," I said.

"Oh yes." She laughed. "It's here on the driver's license."

I nodded.

She set to work typing on the keyboard—with one finger.

I was already regretting having left my phone in the car. And there was nothing interesting blaring from the TV set. I turned back to her, pecking away.

She stopped abruptly and looked at me, petrified. "You're a gold member," she said in what could easily be interpreted as an awed, somewhat timid voice.

"Yes." I nodded with a slight smile, somewhere between perturbed and amused.

She returned to her pecking, hunching more closely to the screen. "Can I see your card?" she asked.

I looked at my card, which was on her counter next to her arm. She caught my gaze, followed it, and then emitted a high, nervous, laugh. She swiped my card and then frowned at the screen. "It didn't go through," she said out loud to no one. She was about to swipe it again, and then turned it over. "I had it upside down." She smiled sheepishly.

She swiped the card again and read the computer screen. Then she handed me back my license and card but with some hesitancy.

It dawned on me that she was reading prompts. She did seem to have read my mind. "You're the first guest I've ever checked in. It's my first night."

I nodded, feeling curiously both more and less tired at exactly the same time.

Then she added, "There's coffee over there. This might take a while."

"I'm good," I responded. And it did take a while. Three attempts to swipe my card. Two attempts to program the room key. Over a minute to write the room number on the back of the card that holds the room key. (She had to look at the screen twice.) "It's down the hall and to the...." She stuck out her right hand, pointed right and then—left. "Left."

I didn't say anything. Figuring it out on my own would be faster, I was sure.

But then I did ask, "Where is the best parking?" This was undoubtedly a mistake, but I was in this far.

She hesitated, thinking.

"Is there parking behind the building?" I prompted. "Near an entrance?"

"Yes," she responded with confidence. "That's where my car is."

So we were now the only two cars parked in the back. "Great. I'll pull around then."

She nodded. Then she remembered. "Breakfast is complimentary and from 7:00 to 10:00."

I looked at her. "Tomorrow's Friday so it should be 6:00 to 9:30, right?"

Her eyes got big, and I smiled.

Fortunately, she smiled back. "You know this better than I do." She laughed.

"Well, I've done this more than once. You'll be fine. I'm sure it gets easier. Oh, the fitness center is open 24 hours and the pool closed at 11:00, right?"

"I'm sure you're right." She looked relieved. "Have a good evening."

It was now 21 minutes after I first approached the desk. "Thank you. And you're welcome," I replied.

After I drove around back, got my bags out of the car, and got inside, I noticed that the complimentary bottle of water she was supposed to have given me was sitting outside my door.

I suspect I'll never see this woman again, though I feel an odd kinship toward her. Sometimes all you can do is hang on and ride out the storm together.

I don't know which was more satisfying – (1) winning our 4.5 40-and-over tennis match today 6-4, 1-6, 6-0, or (2) having one of our opponents say, "I've never lost a set 6-0 before I played with Keith."

There's another Keith in our league, and we're complete opposites. The other Keith is tall. I'm fat. He's aggressive. I'm consistent. He only thinks when he talks. I only think when I'm quiet. He plays quickly. I play deliberately. He hits hard. I hit angles. When we win the point, he says, "That's because it's Sunday and I'm playing with a minister."

I say, "Sorry. That was lucky."

He calls us the Wonder Twins and wants to fist bump after every good shot. And mostly, with all these differences between us, we just seem to complement each other and have a great time. And the hallmark of any good team, doubles or otherwise: we can laugh—together.

After tennis, Adam and I went for a bite to eat. I ordered an iced tea. Adam looked at the sugar container and asked me, "Is that enough?"

"It's enough for now," I said.

The server eyed us, and Adam patiently explained, "He goes through a lot of sweetener."

I mentioned that there were lots of empty tables around and I would be fine.

The server nodded, took Adam's drink order, and left. When she came back, she had his drink, my iced tea, and at least 20 sweetener packets.

We all laughed, but it felt so nice.

Although it seemed to take forever for the food to come, I didn't mind very much because I felt so good, so cared for. This might have seemed insignificant to someone else. But to me, being heard may be the greatest gift.

I awoke with a start. I thought at first I had missed my plane. I could easily have gone back to sleep, but I forced myself to get up and get going. I jammed my phone, wallet, and iPod into my pocket and headed out. When I arrived at the airport and pulled out my ID to give to the airline agent, I realized I had handed him my passport card. When I put the card back in my wallet, I double-checked that I did have my driver's license. I put my baggage on the conveyor belt with my hat, wallet, and phone in my backpack, and breezed through.

Once I got settled in on the plane, I looked in my backpack for my iPod. But I was thwarted. Sleep won. I woke up when we touched down in Baltimore. It seemed to take forever to deplane, but eventually I was able to head for my favorite breakfast at my favorite diner.

I asked for an iced tea with no lemon and got the tea moments later with two lemon wedges. I wondered if the server had only half paid attention, though she clearly noticed that I took the lemon wedges out and set them aside. Later, after I ordered, she did a double take when she saw the empty sweetener packets piled like a small ski slope next to the under-appreciated lemon wedges. When she brought my breakfast, she also brought another iced tea, and this time sweetener packets instead of lemon, thereby earning her tip.

Once I got situated on my next plane, I decided to look more thoroughly for my iPod. It was not in the backpack. I did find there my little bottle of congestion medicine and realized that TSA had not found it in the screening process. Perhaps it was too small. But I still remembered the time when I'd forgotten a bottle of iced tea and TSA had searched every inch of my body even though that bottle was in my backpack.

I wondered if the iPod was in my roller board, or maybe I had left it on the counter in my kitchen. Disappointing, but I would deal with it later. I settled in for my nap and then wondered where my phone was. It was not in my pocket. Was it still in my backpack? I had just checked there for the iPod. My heart quickened. I felt my pocket again. And then my other pocket where my wallet was.

My iPod was there. It must have been there right along, even when I walked through the screening detector at TSA. And then I remembered I was wearing cargo pants with four pockets and my phone must be in a lower pocket, which it was.

But then I wondered how I made it through TSA with a bottle of liquid in my backpack and my iPod in my pocket. It kept me awake long enough to make it through the exit row briefing, which I know so well I could give it myself. And then I found some music. And then I was out.

When I got off the plane in Rochester and made my way down to baggage claim, nothing was coming off the belt. I noticed my rental car counter was unoccupied so I sauntered down to claim my keys. I handed the agent my license, which she looked at and then handed back to me. I almost thought I'd handed her my passport card, but a quick glance showed me I hadn't.

As I was dealing with getting my luggage into the rental car, something was gnawing at me. Why had I thought my license was a passport card? I had gotten the new license only when an airport agent told me the license I handed over was expired. Had I taken the expired license out of my wallet and kept just the new one? I found the passport card first and put it back. I pulled out the license next. I looked at it a little more closely. Rhode Island reuses pictures from old driver's licenses. I thought I looked young. And then I realized this was my old license. I made sure I didn't also have the new one. But I had been certain the old one was in my kitchen.

And then I laughed. This was my old license. My new one had to be in my kitchen. And five TSA agents, four hotel clerks, and four car rental agents had not noticed over the whole previous month that this was an expired license. But until now, neither had I.

It makes me wonder how much of life we miss because we go through the motions. How much of what we do is out of such habit that we cut corners? Fourteen people, including me, had not noticed that this was my expired license.

Now I would spend the rest of my time in New York driving below the speed limit and obeying all traffic signs and lights. And I would ponder how I missed for over a month what license this was, and how people trained to look for these things missed this as well.

I was sure there was a lesson here, but I would likely remain oblivious and just keep doing what I do—until I got home, where I would trade the licenses first thing. Assuming, of course, that I would remember.

Every time I wonder about the state the world has gotten into, I'm reminded to trust again. Today my assistant, Margaret, and I went to lunch. I took a legal pad with my To Do list on it. After lunch I went back to the office and spent the afternoon taking care of things. Then I looked for my legal pad and realized I had left it at the restaurant. Before catching the train, I rushed back there. I asked the hostess about it, and she immediately brought it out. "We knew you'd come back for it," she said.

Then later, when I was standing by the door of the train, waiting to exit, a woman tapped my shoulder and asked, "Could your cell phone be back on a seat? Did it fall out of your pocket?"

I felt my pockets. Sure enough. No cell phone. I dashed back and there it was on the seat.

I thanked the woman profusely, but she brushed me off. "It's what we each would want someone to do for us. You'll do it for someone else next time."

At breakfast in the Baltimore airport, I was apparently the only witness to the server's pirouette as she went to place an order. But she did see me noticing. I quickly scrawled out "SWE" (for Sweden) on a napkin, and then below it, as if I were a Swedish judge, I wrote her score, "5.8." She bowed, blew me a kiss, and turned to enter the order. And it seems I never got charged for my hash browns.

It was the kind of day where I got in from tennis, kicked off my coat and shoes, got into shorts, and then realized my phone was still in the car. So I slipped on shoes and a coat and ran and got it.

It was the kind of day where I got out the recycling only to find the bin full so I managed to take each item and find a place for it in the bin—in the cold and wind.

It was the kind of day where I sat down to write one short thing and nine and a half pages later realized I was done. And then realized it was four hours later.

It was the kind of day where I finally sat down to enjoy some ice cream—and then managed to spill much of it on my sweatshirt.

I made the best of it. Because some days you get to sprint, some days you get to walk, and some days you get to hurdle.

On a break from first round of interviews for the Transitions Administrator position, I took myself to lunch in a driving rainstorm. It was well worth it, as I went to my favorite restaurant.

I was greeted and placed at a barstool table, where Sam (short for Samantha) showed up with a smile, iced tea, and a whole lot of sweetener. She knows me well. I placed my food order without looking at the menu. I didn't need to.

Marcus brought the gluten-free pizza and noticed I was working on something.

"You must be an editor," he said. I told him I was rewriting a handbook. He said he'd just had something published online, and he invited me to enjoy the pizza.

Sam checked back twice to make sure everything was all right and showed up with a complimentary burrata (cheese with avocado, tomatoes, and other veggies). She said the chef had sent it over.

A few minutes later Marcus checked back and asked about the pizza. I told him it was delicious as always. Then he asked how the burrata was. And then I asked about what he had written.

He brushed it off. "It's nothing. It was my first piece. It was about going hiking and camping with friends and what I learned." He looked at my pile of paper and asked what I was writing.

I told him it was a handbook for congregations on how to conduct a search for a new minister. He brightened and said religion fascinated him. He said he was thinking about atheists and agnostics and very religious people.

I said that atheists had a lot in common with fundamentalists, because both could be rigid in their thinking, and that agnostics were least like the other two. He nodded vigorously. We talked about that for a minute, and he was clearly intrigued by this idea.

I asked him what he had learned from hiking. Mainly I was just enjoying how engaged he was in the conversation.

He dismissed my question. "It was nothing really. I wrote about four things I learned."

"What were they?"

He paused for a minute and then said, "Number one was not to go it alone. Number two was to know your limits and don't have pie-in-the-sky expectations. Number three was to push yourself beyond your limits, if that makes sense."

I nodded. "That's the difference between dreaming too big and pushing yourself a bit."

He grinned. "Exactly." And the fourth was something Eisenhower said. I think it was along the lines of, plans are worthless, but planning is essential. He concluded, "Have a plan even though things won't happen like you planned because having the plan still helped."

I smiled. "Those four things could be in my handbook on how to find a minister. Good advice."

He beamed back at me, and then he realized he had a customer's credit card in his hand. "I have to go run this. I'd love to talk more."

"Of course, go. But if you get caught up, we can talk the next time I'm in for lunch."

"Thanks," he said.

"Thank you," I replied. And he sped off.

Sam came over a minute later to see if I was done and if she could tempt me with a dessert.

When she brought me the check, she said, "You and Marcus talked for a while. I was getting worried for his customers."

"I'm sorry," I said. "We got to talking about his hiking article and how what he wrote fits right in with the handbook I'm writing on how to find a minister."

Her eyes lit up. "Thank you. He really needed that."

"I needed that too," I said.

"Come back soon," she said.

"Count on it," I replied, as she walked away and waved.

And as I headed toward the door, full and content, Marcus waved me out into the afternoon as he took an order at a table for six.

It was probably my favorite meal all week.

I went with a colleague for lunch today, back to the same restaurant as last week. Sure enough, there was Marcus.

He took us to our table, and I told him I'd found online the article he wrote. He gave a start and said it was his first publication. I told him it was good and contained information I could use. He flushed, clearly embarrassed, and also flattered.

He asked if I was an editor, and I reminded him I am a minister and was re-writing a handbook. He nodded, remembering. He asked my colleague what she did, and she said she was a minister too. I could tell he wanted to ask questions, but instead he took our order.

My colleague and I had a lively conversation over salad, and Marcus kept me well stocked with iced tea and sweetener. After the meal and great conversation, he surprised us with gluten-free chocolate chip cookies, which were delicious and gave me quite the sugar buzz. They were on the house, he said.

My colleague said, "He really likes you."

I responded, "I was nice to him. He could be my son. I paid attention."

She nodded and talked about kindness. We agreed it was really so simple, yet these days it often seemed hard.

It was a nice way to end the work week. A great lunch with a colleague where we got to talk about all kinds of good things, making someone's Friday better, a gorgeous day, and good food.

My only regret was the sugar buzz from the chocolate chip cookies. It lasted several hours. But it's a regret I'd gladly repeat.

I didn't get a lot of work done this afternoon. But perhaps that doesn't matter. I think in the end we'll remember—and be remembered for—more whom we cared about, and less what we did. We think we don't have time to pay attention. I think we don't have time not to pay attention. In my mind, that's what our world needs. People over commodities. Connections over things. Honoring another's story, however simple they might think it is.

Tennis can be a great teacher. When I get going forward, and stay balanced with small quick steps, get my knees bent, and keep my focus on the ball, I play really well. I also know where the ball is going with greater reliability.

I've learned that even when I'm not playing tennis, when I meet things head on, stay on my toes, and stay agile and focused, I feel better. I have a better sense of what to overlook.

Sometimes the simplest things are the first things forgotten and lost, which ultimately makes things harder.

Some people think I play tennis to whack balls and let go of emotion. There probably is some truth to that. Some of it is just joy. And a lot of it is about reminding myself how simple things matter and help.

Tonight was a good tennis night. I could also call it a better life night.

The most Zen shot in tennis for me is the overhead smash. The less I work at it, the more I do it well. For many people, it is a very hard shot to learn. No one really taught it to me. I just watched Pete Sampras and Martina Navratilova hit their overheads. Often the harder the overhead, the more I relax and do the basics.

Yet how often is the hard thing harder because we are so anxious that we don't do the simple parts!

Today was a long, hard day of work. Lots of details to attend to. Yet I just tried to breathe and keep moving. The end of the ministerial search cycle can be very hard for everyone involved—ministers, congregational leaders, and everyone involved in administering the process, including the Transitions Director, that is, me.

I got to hit overheads at tennis tonight. I missed several of my first ones, and then I reminded myself to breathe and try less hard, to just do it and let the moment happen, let the muscle memory take over, just focus on the ball.

It was therapeutic. Therapeutic just to move. Therapeutic just to breathe. Therapeutic to stop trying so hard and just do. Therapeutic not to hit the ball hard but to hit a smart shot with the angle that was harder to get.

I realized I was really tired at the end of tennis. But less tired than before tennis after running around for 90 minutes of trying to get a whole lot of things done.

It made it easier to come back to some necessary work after tennis. I was more thoughtful, less anxious.

It made me wonder what other people's overhead is. And what are the other things we do that allow us to shift gears, find a less hectic pace, and just be focused on the ball? So I'm grateful for overhead smashes tonight. And the chance to hit a few of them without trying.

My train into Eugene, Oregon, got in much later than expected. I took a cab to get the rental car. The driver, about 30, was a student of African-Asian descent. It turned out he was from Cambridge, Massachusetts. He had been in this country three and a half years, and he was studying to become a chiropractor. He was interested to hear that I live in New England, in Providence, Rhode Island.

A driver cut him off and skipped over two lanes. "Man," he lamented.

"If this were New England, that would be normal," I replied.

He laughed. "There isn't anything normal here," he said.

"What do you mean?"

"Well, you can't get Indian food here. It says it's Indian food, but there's no spice to anything. I like Indian food hot."

That made me wonder, so I wondered out loud. "How diverse is it here? Surely the University of Oregon brings in diverse students."

"Most of the African Americans are athletes here. There are Asian people here, but it's 99% Chinese. But the white people...." he began and looked at me through the rearview mirror.

I smiled. "What about them? All old hippies, right?"

He laughed. "This town has the most diverse white people of anywhere I've been."

That made me laugh. "How are they diverse?"

"There are more kinds of beer here than people of color. And there are more different types of weed."

We had nearly talked ourselves to the airport. He dropped me off, and while I was signing the credit card voucher, he unloaded the taxi.

I extended my hand. He took it and pulled me into a hug. "Thanks for talking to me, man. Thanks for listening."

I was both a bit surprised and also a bit sad. This was an interesting guy. Did he really have no one who would listen to him?

"You too," I said. "Good luck with school."

"I'll be the first doctor in my family." He brightened. He smiled and waved as he got into his taxi.

Suddenly I was no longer the tired traveler I was earlier. I had a little more hope, thinking of this man taking the initiative to pursue his dreams.

Tonight at the grocery store, I was getting just a few things. This burly guy, probably an EMT, was sweating over flowers, chocolates, and Valentine's Day cards. This was clearly not something he does every day or lightly. I was impressed that he had pored over at least 20 cards, reading each one. He was either very happy or in the doghouse, probably the basement of the doghouse, given his brow.

I finally found the electronic cord I was looking for and moved on to gather some guacamole and hummus.

Once I had all my stuff, I headed toward the check-out. The burly EMT was in line as I approached. He realized he'd forgotten something and rushed back.

The evening cashier, Jeanne, whom I often see after tennis, was still holding the flowers. She nodded as I approached and laid my groceries on the conveyor belt.

The EMT was rushing back, and I caught Jeanne's wink.

"Happy Valentine's Day," she said to me when the EMT was in earshot. He stopped, clearly surprised.

"For me?" I said. "How thoughtful of you!"

The EMT looked first at Jeanne and then at me to see if we were joking.

"We see each other at least twice a week," I told him. "We're pretty discreet. But since it's Valentine's Day, we've decided to come clean. Isn't she thoughtful?"

He looked at me, wide-eyed, wanting to believe I was joking. Then he looked at Jeanne, who batted her eyes. (I'm guessing she's on at least her 65th journey around the sun.) She broke into laughter, and we all joined in.

It made my night, and I hope hers and the EMT's as well.

He paid, then grinned at Jeanne and then at me. We wished him Happy Valentine's Day, and he walked off.

Jeanne looked at me and held out her hand for a high five.

I returned it, and we chuckled together as she totaled my items.

Even though it wasn't quite Valentine's Day, this may have been my favorite Valentine ever.

What Really Matters

PART TWO

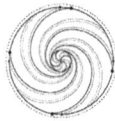

When They Find Out
You Are a Minister

What Really Matters

I made a quick run to the store today.

I went to check out with a few items and the cashier said, "Hi Keith. How are you today?"

Now I've been to this town any number of times over the years and I was thinking this was probably a classmate of one of my friends. Did I know him through the local church? Was this another General Assembly attendee who had escaped 4,000 of their friends for a moment? Should I fake it or come clean?

"I'm okay. A bit tired. Remind me where I know you from?"

"I've never met you before," he replied. "I just read your name tag on your chest."

I realized I was still wearing my Unitarian Universalist Association name tag.

"Are you really a minister?" he asked.

"Yes."

"I didn't think ministers were allowed to wear tennis shoes."

I tried not to laugh. But I managed to say without cracking up, "Casual Saturday."

He did a slight double-take, and I just smiled. He rang up the tennis balls I had purchased. "And ministers can play tennis too?"

"If you pray between serves, it's allowed."

He laughed, though the true fun was because he was still not convinced I was teasing him. "Are you a good tennis player?"

"Well, my team went to nationals last year. I've taught kids how to play tennis. I even own five tennis racquets."

"Wow!" He paused. "You can own five tennis racquets."

"Yes. I had to ask special permission."

The poor guy was completely baffled, and I was milking this for all it was worth. "I even drink holy water on the change-overs."

He stared at me and finally asked, "Really?"

"No, I'm teasing you. Gatorade is better for you than holy water."

I laughed, and then he realized finally that I had been teasing him all along.

He smiled sheepishly. "I've had a long day."

"I have too," I said. "Thanks for letting me tease you. This will make for a great story in a sermon."

He stared at me. "No way."

I laughed. "Actually I'm telling the truth on that one."

He was quiet for a second.

"We can find religion in everyday life," I said.

I feared his head would explode, but he finally grinned and then laughed. He handed me my receipt and said, "Have a good night."

"Thank you," I said. "I am having one now. You have a good night too." And I smiled and walked to the car, not quite as tired as I had been all day.

I did take-out tonight since the Patriots were going to be on. I showed up and got my steak, steak fries, and green beans. I had paid online, which the clerk had forgotten until I told her.

Clearly she was a bit rattled after she checked her register, which confirmed that I had paid. She apologized profusely, and I told her not to worry. But when I told her I'm a minister, she got more flustered. She pulled out real silverware to give me instead of plastic, though she caught herself as she went to put it in my bag.

Then, for the cherry on top, when she asked if I wanted the receipt put in the bag or handed to me and I said in the bag, she nodded and proceeded to put her wallet in my bag.

I couldn't resist. "Are you making a donation to the church?"

She was startled, and I pointed next to the register where she'd put the receipt. Then I pulled her wallet out of the bag.

Looking mortified, she took it from me and managed a thank you in a quiet tone.

I smiled. "You did better than many," I said. "I had one woman give out a little scream some time ago when I told her I was a minister. And she was only serving chicken wings."

The absurdity of statement worked. She lightened up and finally laughed.

I wished her good night and hoped aloud that the rest of her evening would be clergy free.

She giggled and smiled, and I noticed her shoulders relax. She handed me the bag and thanked me.

I grinned. As I went out the door, I said, "Just be ready. I'll be back tomorrow to be sure you have the restaurant minimum of six free giveaways." She was laughing harder now, which I heard and enjoyed all the way to my car.

"Why do you have so many bags?" the border agent asked as I rolled up with a large suitcase, which was supporting a large green duffel bag. I had my smaller duffel and my backpack over my shoulder.

"I'm the world's worst packer," I replied, and she failed to mask a growing grin.

"What's in your backpack?" she asked.

"My laptop, work, books."

"Can I open it?"

I thought, she's the Customs official and is in control here, but I nodded and said, "Sure."

She tried to open the backpack but then realized she had hold of the zipper where the straps come out. Eventually she found all the zippers and saw inside all the backpack areas. "This a great backpack," she remarked.

I told her I love it.

She eyed the other three bags. "What's in the duffel bags?"

"Iced tea," I deadpanned.

She stopped and looked at me. Eventually, she asked, "Why?"

"You don't sell this brand here in Canada. Here take a look." I was amused.

She unzipped the duffel and stopped short. She looked around in the bag. "They're plastic."

Observant, I thought sarcastically. She must be good at her job. I didn't say that out loud, of course.

"What about the other duffel bag?"

"The same," I replied. "Also some protein bars."

She eyed me again, and I could tell she was thinking something she really shouldn't say. I put the duffel up for her to see, and she opened it—and stopped again.

I smiled back, my grin growing large.

She finally came up with a question. Where was I going and how long would I be in Canada?

I told her about the train trip I had planned.

She was figuring something out. "That's about eight iced teas a day."

"I hope that will tide me over."

She found the sweetener packets as I was saying this. She appeared to be figuring out whether pursuing this would be worth it. She quickly reached the conclusion to that question and asked, "What do you do for work?"

I told her I'm a Unitarian Universalist minister.

She just nodded, somewhat defeated. "That's a religion?" she asked.

I told her, "Yes."

The light had gone from her eyes. My 60 bottles of tea and 400 packets of sweetener had worn her down. This was evidenced by her last question: "Any guns or other weapons?"

I was aghast, if in a subdued way. "No, I'm a minister," I said, the slightest whiff of outrage in my voice.

She shook her head, nodded numbly, then paused, closing her eyes. "Have a great trip," she said with resignation in her voice.

I nodded vigorously. The upper hand was all mine. "I already am having one." I smiled, though it was clear she didn't realize I said this at her expense.

I gathered my bags and rolled slowly out of Customs. I looked over my shoulder to see that she had watched me leave, shaking her head.

Crossing the border has rarely been this much fun.

I went to a tennis academy for a couple of days of drills. One of the pros, who normally worked with the juniors, was surprised to learn I was a minister. "I'd love to talk to you," she said. We found a few minutes after the morning session, and I discovered that what she really wanted was a confessional. She told me the hardest thing about working with juniors was not the students but the parents. She looked at me. "One parent is always crazy," she said.

I nodded.

"And it takes a toll on the kids. They are pushed and pushed and pushed, and they lose their joy in the sport."

I thought of a friend of mine who tells me he hates to play because he always hears his mother's voice in his head when he misses a shot.

"And the truth is," the pro continued, "most of these players are going to end up like me—a coach, a pro, but not someone who makes the tour."

I looked at her. "Do you like what you do?" I asked.

She smiled. "Most of the time."

"Do you show these kids that? It would be important for them to see. I mean hitting with you made me happy this morning. Quite happy."

She laughed. "Thanks," she said.

I told her there are times when I wish I had been raised like her students, but then I also wondered if I'd enjoy tennis now as much if I had been. I told her that the only voice in my head was my own.

She told me she wished I worked there with her, and I said they probably did need a chaplain there.

She laughed and said she had to get back to the juniors but she felt like she should write me a check instead of me paying for tennis. That made me laugh, and she gave me a quick hug. Funny how you remember moments like that.

PART THREE

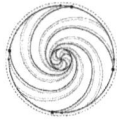

What Were
They Thinking?

What Really Matters

In Canada, I always stop to get tuna because they have sun-dried tomato and basil flavored tuna in small snack cans—cheap—$1.27 CDN, way less than in the States, assuming you can find them here at all. In the US, if you can find them, they are $3.00 a can with crackers. Today I stopped and got 20 cans.

Today, of course, would be the day that Customs was checking every car. I spent an hour in the tunnel under the Detroit River with no radio connection. But eventually I got to the Customs station.

One agent asked where I'd been as another agent and a German Shepard approached the back of the car.

The first agent asked where I was from, and I told him I was from Rhode Island but working with a congregation in Kingsville. That produced a moment of hesitation. But he recovered and asked if I had bought anything.

I told him I stopped and got some books. And some tuna fish at the grocery store.

He looked at me. "Pop the trunk." Which I did.

"He says he has books and tuna from Canada," he yelled back to the other agent. I was sure the German Shepard was already on it.

"Why tuna?" the first agent asked. By then I had lost sight of the other agent and the dog.

"Hard to find in the US. Cheap here. And tasty."

He eyed me with a look of what may best be described as incredulity. So much for the inscrutable border agent.

The other agent walked forward with the grocery bag. "This is for real. He has 20 cans of tuna." The Shepard was sniffing hopefully.

"Should we check out a can?" the first agent asked.

"There should be a receipt in the bag," I offered.

The second agent fished through the bag and pulled out the receipt. "Twenty cans. Wow. Looks like he did come to Canada for tuna fish," he said and handed the bag to the first agent, who looked inside.

"You stopped at a store for tuna?" the first agent asked.

"Well, they didn't have mini sweetener packets, or I'd have gotten those too."

"What?" the first agent asked.

"Oh, I get those," said the second agent. "Keeps you from looking like a cocaine addict."

The first agent looked bewildered.

"Instead of packets, which spill, you get a small plastic dispenser and the sweetener is in small pills. Two pills equal one packet. Without the mess."

A double take. Then a recovery. "Anything else back there?"

The second agent said, "Yeah a lot of books. I wanted to read a couple. Especially the children's book on microbes. Who knew there was such a thing?" Then he realized the first agent was staring at him. "My son would love that book," he offered somewhat feebly. "There's a lot of luggage back there, but he's fine."

The first agent nodded and handed me back my passport and tuna. "As soon as he closes the trunk, you're free to go. Have a nice day. Enjoy your tuna—and microbes."

I laughed all the way to the interstate, fairly sure that was a statement never said by a Customs agent before.

To take a break from work today, I drove a friend currently without a car to the outlet malls in Wrentham so he could get a coat. He didn't find one.

I found a coat. I also found two tennis warm-up pullovers, a new pair of sweats, a new shirt, and a children's book.

He ended up buying a coat online. For $500. I got my haul for about $135.

My favorite moment was in the coat store where my friend almost bought a coat. While he was trying on various coats, I saw one that caught my eye. It looked smart and just right for those 30-degree days. A little dressier than I'd normally get, but definitely worth a look.

I examined it, and I could see out of the corner of my eye that the salesperson on the floor was eyeing me, appraising me in my slightly tattered Colgate sweatshirt and somewhat stained olive cargo pants. I thought the coat certainly wouldn't fit in my pocket. Did she think I was going to shoplift a coat I liked but didn't love? I tried it on, and it had a good fit. But I had just bought a coat that should serve me well. And on sale that coat had been a great bargain at $45.

Still a little retail therapy could be good. I returned to the coat, thinking I liked it but didn't love it. The price might help me love it or forget it.

I found the tag and I realized I had today's Scoreboard Stumper: Why was a $1,295 coat even being sold in an outlet mall next to a toy store that was selling everything at 50% off? It was the same mall where I got the children's book marked at $5.95 but really $2.98 after the 50% markdown.

I was so stunned by the price of the coat that it slipped off my shoulder and hit the floor.

I heard the salesperson gasp.

She rushed toward me and picked the coat up with a reverence that was palpable and gave me a look of genuine disdain.

I apologized to the glare on the salesperson's face and moved toward an open area, where I didn't feel like I could touch anything.

And I didn't.

When my friend came out of the fitting room, saying he didn't like any of the coats, I told him I tried one too that I didn't love. He commiserated with me on account of my not loving the house down payment masquerading as a winter jacket. He then launched into a bit of a tirade about the importance of belt loops on coats.

My mind wandered. I longed for the sporting goods store, where the world makes sense and you can buy six pair of white athletic crew socks for $11.95 and feel like you've paid too much.

We were followed out of the coat store by a glare. I'm sure I had committed at least one of their seven deadly sins.

Still, it got me out of the house. And I was sure they would forget who I was by next year.

I was in the convenience store tonight, looking at trial-sized toiletries. A woman with a basket walked up and stood right in front of me as if I were not there. And then she began to walk back and forth in front of me.

A man who had been looking at mouthwash started looking at both of us. His eyes got big. I just gave him a smile.

Eventually the woman left, never having acknowledged my presence. I picked up some shampoo, went off to get a few other things, and then headed for the check-out.

The man from the toiletries counter pulled his cart up behind me. "I can't believe she did that," he said.

I smiled. "It takes a special kind of talent to be that oblivious of others."

He laughed.

I'm just glad I had a witness.

After getting off the train tonight, I was walking behind a woman on my way to my car in the parking lot. I pulled out my keys, hit the button, and popped the trunk.

The woman took off her backpack and put in my trunk.

"Ummm, excuse me," I said, "this is my car."

She immediately became angry. "No, it's my car."

I decided she clearly was confused. "Okay," I said, "what's your license number?"

She looked down at my plate and swore loudly. "I'm sorry," she said sheepishly.

I just laughed. "It's okay," I said.

She removed her backpack without a word.

It's amazing how much we can retreat into our own little world.

Instead of getting into my car, I walked to the neighborhood rip-off gas station and convenience store down the street. Partly I wanted to get my day's required number of steps in. So I paid $5.99 for a large box of cereal.

But the milk—oh, the milk. It wasn't the price. Though it was high. But I wanted a small bottle. I'd get more on my next trip to the grocery store.

A slim bottle seemed like the best idea. But I noticed the expiration date was the day before. I decided not to chance it. I could splurge on a larger size.

Skim milk's expiration date for a mid-size bottle was a week and a half earlier. Every bottle, five of them, had the same date. I did look for curdles. Not yet, but....

So I got 1%, which wouldn't expire for five more days. A small bottle. But I let the clerk know.

"Oh, well, I don't drink milk," he said.

It took me a minute to realize he was serious. And clueless.

"It's probably why no one has bought any," I said.

He nodded.

"Has no one told you this earlier?"

"Yeah, you're the second guy today," he said, working the cash register scanner on my expensive cereal and 1% milk.

I was annoyed, but he was so nonplussed about it all that I got curious. "Do you have a pool going on when the 10th person says it?"

"I don't think so," he said slowly.

"Well, put me down for Monday at two o'clock then."

He eyed me for a moment and then said with ever so slight a smile, "What will you buy if you win?"

I collected my change and cereal and the 1% milk. "I'll buy fresh milk," I said. "Just not all at once."

I didn't wait to find out if I would I hear laughter. I was out the door, at least 2% more annoyed than when I entered. But at least I had cereal. Some days you take what you can get.

There were people from five flights clamoring to collect baggage at the same time. Children running, babies crying, adults talking loudly into their phones or to elderly parents and children who needed sleep and were fighting it. And then out of the blue, a woman glided through the din of the mob. She didn't hush the crowd but at least lowered the level of pandemonium. Heads turned.

She was wearing a pair of old shorts, no-show socks, unicorn slippers—yes, that's right—complete with their singular horn covered in glitter, and a tee shirt that read, "Yes, they're real!" It was a toss-up whether this referred to the slippers or, well, something else.

As this woman paraded past the baggage claim, another woman who had uncrated her two overly styled terriers complete with bows and a sense of superiority, stood in the path of the unicorns and the woman wearing them. The terriers sniffed at the horns, glitter, and off-white fuzz. And then, to their owner's horror, they took aim. Thwarted by a quick pull of the leash, the terriers yelped at their loss of privilege and glared momentarily at their owner.

The unicorns right-turned their escape into the ladies' rest room, and a slight tittering swelled from the crowd. Above the noise, one could hear the canned music in the background. The lyrics rang out, "Silent night/Holy Night/All is calm/All is bright."

I dropped my wallet in South Station. A guy picked it up and handed it to me. He was two steps behind me. He said, "Is there a finder's fee?"

I said, "Thank you."

He repeated, "Is there a finder's fee?"

I smiled at him.

"You should give me $5."

I just looked at him, appalled.

He said, "Next time, I'll just keep it."

I was more appalled, and still am.

When I went to the rest room on the plane, I left on my seat the book I had been reading. It was about church dynamics.

The young woman in the window seat drinking a Mimosa apparently looked at the book while I was gone. When I returned, it was in a different spot from where I had left it. I smiled and sat down, picking up my book. She smiled back, gulped her drink, and closed her eyes.

When the flight attendant came down the aisle collecting trash, the young woman asked for another Mimosa.

A moment later, with drink sipped and in hand, the young woman reached over and touched my arm. "Can I ask you a question?"

I nodded, and then she laughed. "I guess I mean, can I ask you two questions since I just asked you one?"

We both smiled.

"Do you think any man could have an emotional affair without acting on it sexually?"

My mind raced. How could I answer succinctly and forthrightly in a way that meant I had heard her without getting myself burdened with a story that I knew was there?

She looked at me expectantly, while I paused for a second considering, though it felt like both 15 minutes and a nanosecond.

"Sure," I replied, and left it there.

"Thank you," she said, with some relief and a nod.

I nodded back, then waited for an interminable five seconds before returning to my book.

She gulped her drink and then closed her eyes, resting her head against the window.

We landed 20 minutes later. After I got my bags, as I was heading out to the rental car, there was the young woman, on the phone, all smiles. She beamed at me and waved her free hand wildly. I waved back, way more feebly, and headed to my car. I was hoping I had helped her out.

On the other hand, I suppose I should have thanked her too, since our encounter led to my making up a whole lot of stories. But I suspect her reality was as adventurous as my mind. So I said a prayer of gratitude for being boring at the moment, and a prayer of protectiveness, in case my one-word guess, "Sure," led to an unfortunate outcome. I was afraid that word suggested to her a whole lot more than it meant to me when I said it.

But I think potential implications carry weight only for a moment. She will know the full meaning of an answer to her question only if she asks directly.

I do hope she's not flying back next Saturday.

I was delayed in St. Louis getting to Lincoln, Nebraska. The airline gave each passenger a $100 voucher. The odd thing was that we left less than an hour after the scheduled time. You'd have thought that would have mollified everyone. Alas, though most were happy, not all.

I decided, since it was a short trip, to do what was unusual for me. I took a window seat. It would be easier to nap on this short flight.

I fell asleep almost immediately, until a woman threw her purse into the seat next to me and it crashed into my arm, which was resting on the armrest.

When I opened my eyes, the woman was glaring at the flight attendant. Then she turned to her husband, who had the aisle seat across the aisle. "I don't care if it's $100. I'm not flying this rinky-dink airline again, making us late like this."

I looked at the husband, and it was hard not to have sympathy for him because clearly this was not the first rant he'd been present for.

It also gave me an idea why the couple chose to sit across the aisle from each other instead of next to each other.

The woman suddenly noticed her purse next to me and grabbed it, clearly afraid I would take something out of it.

"That's where it landed when you placed it there," I said. "It woke me up."

She glared it me. "Well, I'm going to leave it there," she said, "I don't believe them when they say the plane is full." And then she actually said, "I deserve some space."

I decided my best option was to go back to sleep, so I did, and, thankfully, quickly. I woke up about half an hour into the flight though, with the poor guy who now occupied the middle seat leaning into me, and clearly away from her. "It's a short flight," I whispered.

"Not short enough," he whispered back, and we broke into smiles.

The woman was clearly partaking of an adult beverage and was still scowling. I can't recall the last time I was that happy to be tired.

I never truly get away from work. But I did manage not to look at email all day long. And I got in a walk by the shore of Lake Superior, had lunch in a place where the homemade cream of mushroom soup tasted a lot like it came out of a can, and did a bit of writing. I thought I would probably write more the next day since it was supposed to pour all day.

Though maybe instead I would go back to the gift shop with the friendly German Shepard. The owner said from around the corner, "Capone? Did another child walk into the shop?" Then she added, "He loves children." And then she rounded the corner and saw that I was the only one there. She stopped, somewhat taken aback. "Do you have a child?"

"Um, no," I said.

"He's not done that with an adult before. Especially a male adult."

I looked at her for a second and made the mistake of stopping giving Capone—who names their dog Capone?—a shoulder massage. He used his nose to direct my arm back to his shoulders. Needless to say, I sat down and let Capone snuggle next to me.

The owner just shook her head and smiled.

This afternoon I went to the pharmacy to pick up my diabetes prescription. It was being finished, and I was invited to have a seat.

A man came in and sat down across from me. He never approached the counter. But he got mad when a new arrival went up to the counter, and before the new person, a young woman, could speak, the man said sternly, "We were in line next."

I looked at him. "I'm just waiting," I said.

"Well, I was next in line," the man said. He was clearly someone who worked out at a gym. He was wearing a tank top and showing significant biceps. And—a first for me—he had on pink terrycloth gym shorts. I assumed he wanted attention and perhaps was the kind of guy who often begged for a fight.

The young woman look startled and backed away. The man in pink terrycloth gym shorts sat staring angrily for a moment.

The pharmacist called for someone else in the waiting area, and he proceeded to pay and leave.

Another man entered. Before he could approach the counter, Pink Terrycloth Shorts spoke up. "I was in line next." And then in a louder voice, "They texted me that my meds were ready."

The pharmacist looked out from behind the counter at him, wide-eyed. "Can I help you?" she asked.

Pink Terrycloth Shorts said, "You texted me that my meds were ready."

"What's your last name?" the pharmacist asked, and after he answered, she scurried to find his medication.

Another woman walked into the pharmacy, and Pink Terrycloth Shorts told her, "The line starts over there." Then in a loud aside to the rest of us, "I wish people would follow the rules."

I could only imagine that he expected everyone to understand his rules, and it was almost a dare. The pharmacist handed him his medication. He paid and left.

Another pharmacist appeared and apologized to all of us who were waiting. "I'm sorry. He's done that before. We've learned it's best not to engage him."

There were nods all around.

"Well," I said, "I'm grateful he gets that medication from here and that you all make sure he gets it, and I hope I never need the same prescription."

The pharmacist smiled. "Your prescription is ready, Keith."

And then when I went to the counter to pay, she whispered, "No co-payment today, Keith. This one's on us."

After my massage, I got a haircut.

The stylist was interested in my massage. "I've never gotten a massage," she said. "Do they talk to you the entire time?"

"No," I replied.

"Good," she said, "I would just want some peace when someone was working on me." Then she kept talking during my entire haircut.

Here's to the woman in the self-scan 12-item-or-less checkout aisle with 37 items. It was, of course, the line I picked. Let me clarify. It was at least 37 items since I started counting the dings well into her order.

And then, of course, the machine broke down and she needed help. And then she decided she didn't need three items so she returned them and had to have them taken off her total.

No one said anything to her, including me, though she did end up having two employees help her with the machine, and three (yes, three) baggers come help bag her groceries.

I, of course, had counted the number of items I had (11) before getting into the line. And bagged all 11 myself.

For anyone interested in such information, the woman with 37 items was white, well dressed for Labor Day, with a purse that I'm guessing was expensive. And even though it was cloudy all day, she was wearing large sunglasses.

I do wish now I had asked her why she had picked this line. It took me 10 minutes to get eggs and milk and hummus and fruit and cooking spray (my impulse buy was a *TV Guide*), and at least twice that to get out of the line. I did notice that everyone else in a line waiting was on their phone texting or reading. If I'd been smarter, I'd have read the *TV Guide* and saved $4.99.

I was driving today behind a Porsche that was going 15 mph in a 40 mph zone. He anticipated red lights, slowing down as he approached two green lights and waiting for them to turn yellow so he could stop. There were eventually six cars behind him, and at least two drivers honked. I did see him look in his rearview mirror, which confirmed he knew there was a string of cars behind him, and I could see the driver was definitely a man.

It was only when he pulled into a store's parking lot that he changed. He sped up. I heard tires as I went by. I didn't look back, but I wondered what his story was. He didn't seem distracted, and I thought he was just careful, until he wasn't. For a while there, I did debate crossing the double yellow line to pass him, but I didn't do it.

I realize the car has become something of a monastery for many drivers, but whatever monastery he was in, I'd rather not visit.

I am not sure what to make of this encounter, but I have thought about it off and on since it happened this afternoon. I wondered if the man was in pain, from a migraine, for instance, or possibly having fun at all six cars' expense.

The story I eventually settled on was that he had a monitoring device on his Porsche and was keeping his insurance rate low while he kept that woman from the insurance company commercial in the trunk because he was mad at her for conning him into buying that device.

The people at the car rental in San Antonio were trying to be kind. They did not know I am the world's worst packer. But seeing me with a duffel bag, a large rolling bag, a small rolling bag, and an overstuffed backpack, they might have begun to clue in. Still, while I appreciated their generosity, they didn't realize that I actually have learned how to be an expert at dealing with my—um, well—condition.

The car rental representative ran to get me a cart so I could get all four bags from the car to Ticketing and insisted on packing the bags onto the cart for me.

This was a mistake. I offered to do it myself, started to, and was literally told, "That's not how you should do it." The know-it-all then proceeded to put my large rolling bag on first, the small rolling bag next to it, and the duffel bag on top, while the backpack went into the upper basket.

I suppressed a smirk. But I did say, "This will fall."

"No, it won't," he said. "You'll be fine."

Now the experienced over-packer knows that you put the small rolling bag on first, then the large one, then the duffel bag on top. With the angle of the cart, this way all the weight is headed towards the back. The car rental rep didn't seem to get this, but I did appreciate the help.

I decided a lived example was the best teaching method. I took the cart and pushed it forward for all of four steps before the duffel bag toppled forward and off the cart.

The car rental rep moved forward but I waved him off. "I might have done this once or twice before," I said as he stopped.

And then I proceeded to put the bags in the cart using the tried and true Keith Kron Over-Packer Way.

It's only a slight exaggeration to say that he gawked as I easily rolled the cart away. The luggage, of course, was perfectly balanced.

"Amateurs," I said under my breath and disappeared onto the elevator with a wry smile.

And it got better.

I rolled up to the Ticketing counter. The agent asked me to put the heavier bag on the scale. I began to place the duffel on the scale, and she protested. "I said the heavier bag."

I continued to set the duffel down on the scale, and it read "47 lbs."

She made me remove it and put on the large rolling bag.

With unbridled glee, I placed the large rolling bag on the scale.

She did a double take, frowned, and then laughed. "You're good." She smiled.

And I laughed. "I might have a little experience here. Twenty-two years of bad packing does teach you something."

She laughed a little, handed me my boarding pass, and wished me a safe flight.

The TSA Pre-check agent asked me to get my bags after I walked through the sensor and set off the alarm. Then he wanted to know if I had a laptop. I have two. He asked to check them. Now this seemed odd to me since my bags hadn't set off the alarm. I had. But after two incidents already that day, I decided to play along. The laptops checked out fine, and it was only when I got to my gate that I realized that my Bluetooth was still in my pocket. Which they never checked.

Still, there was nothing to be gained by challenging the TSA agent. So I didn't.

And when I got home to Providence and made it to Baggage Claim before realizing I had left my phone in the seat back pocket, I proceeded to the Baggage Claim office and told them where it was. They radioed the gate and recovered the phone, and I was able to get it. Thank goodness, I remembered the row and seat.

"Most people are panicked when they do this," the agent said, with what I decided was awe.

"I might have done this once or twice before," I said. "I was either going to get it back or it was getting a free trip to Baltimore, or someone took it. But given when I remembered, I banked on the first possibility.

"Do you need a hand with your luggage?" she asked as she handed me back the phone.

I smiled. "Trust me. I've got this. Thank you."

She looked dubious but just nodded. I loaded up the bags on the cart, with the small rolling bag first, and rolled away.

After tennis, I went to the store to get a cold gel pack for my wrist. It had rained all day today, and all the carts were wet. I found the driest one I could.

Twenty feet into the store, I realized I had a squeaky wheel.

And so did everyone else. To say I turned heads would be an understatement.

I decided to live with it. I could have gone back and traded, but why? All the carts were wet. My cart was the driest of the ones I'd seen.

Not one but four people said, "Did you know your wheel squeaks?"

To the first three, I just nodded and smiled.

Two people said plainly, "Your wheel squeaks."

What makes people want to state the obvious? Did they assume I hadn't noticed? Couldn't hear?

Should I have said, "No. Thank you for telling me. I'll get the management over here right now"?

By the third person to speak, I wished I knew American Sign Language.

I loved imagining the reaction of people thinking I didn't know my wheel was squeaking and realizing they were talking to a person who couldn't hear them.

I'll remember this for next time. Before then I'll try to learn, "I can't hear you. Let me read your lips" in ASL.

At the end of my January trip, I mailed two boxes of books home—from the same post office at the same time. They were even the same weight—27.36 lbs. each. The postal clerk in Florida was impressed that I had distributed the books so evenly.

One box arrived a week later, February 3.

A week after that first box arrived, I started trying to track the second box. And for two weeks, I got the same message pretty much every day, that it was en route. I found this all very impersonal and demoralizing.

The other box arrived February 24. What I immediately noticed was that it was wrapped in plastic and the box was broken open in several places. I also noticed the box felt light. So I feared the worst.

For good reason.

I weighed the box—7.8 lbs. I opened it and found seven books and lots of brown paper wrinkled up. The other box had 20 books in it.

In the box that was broken open, there was a poorly copied, perfunctory letter of apology that told me I was a "Valued Customer." It also gave me a website address to file a missing claim report. I wondered if it was even worth it.

But I decided I could at least vent on the form. Which I did, after having to give permission for them to send me email promotions. And, of course, I hadn't taken the time to photograph the spines of all the books to be able to log them, so it was pretty much a hopeless exercise.

Shipping each of the seven books in the damaged box cost $2.32, with arrival four weeks after they were mailed.

I did take pictures of the box, including one with it on a scale, and I kept the tracking number. I had half a mind to show up at the post office and ask for a refund of 75%. I wondered how long they knew of the broken box before finally repacking it and sending it on.

But mostly I was annoyed because I love books. They tell stories of value that are not about my life but in some ways become a part of my life and story—at least enriching it. And I remember thinking as I packed those books that it felt like I was mailing myself Christmas presents. I anticipated the joy of opening them, which I did get with the first box.

Somewhere some good books were ruined or lost. And I'll probably never know how or why, even though I'm a "Valued Customer."

This experience brought back to mind my years of teaching school. Sometimes I would hear someone putting a child down or bullying a child, and I would interrupt. Sometimes I would try and make the bully understand, at least make them say they were sorry, but it would just happen again. And the child who was told the other person was sorry, clearly didn't believe it. The other person was saying that only because they had to.

I did wonder how many eyes reviewed the "Valued Customer" letter before it was okayed to be sent out routinely. If one in 10 packages is damaged, as I once read, I can even understand why they would need a form letter.

I have three friends who work for the post office who, I know, work hard. And they have to deal all too often with angry dogs, cranky customers (like me that time), and bad weather.

But I wonder how we can do better—whether it's overworked post office employees, bullies, people who say "I'm sorry" and don't really mean it, or me when I'm having a bad day and miss cues because I'm not paying attention.

To me, saying, "I'm sorry, valued person" isn't enough. The real question is how to get us actually to make amends—not just to apologize but to go out of our way to make things better. We really understand this when we're the "Valued Customer." But how often do we ourselves just send the form letter? How often do we actually show up, engage, and be present to the hurt someone feels? Sometimes hurt that we caused.

I can say this because I know there have been times when I've been the one causing the hurt, and sometimes not even sending the form letter or offering the perfunctory apology with the hope that it's enough.

I did hope the post office would find my books, and I do hope more that we can listen to each other's stories, pay attention, heal what hurts, and strive to be better carriers of boxes of the lives of those around us.

We've all done it.

You scope, appraise, and make your best guess. But you can still find yourself in the wrong check-out line.

I chose the line with two people, avoiding the line where the child in the cart was in full meltdown and the line with the guy buying storage bins, though no two were alike, as well as the line where the woman's cart was so full that I was sure her toilet paper was going to cascade all over the floor around her.

The cashier next to my line opened and she invited me over.

A woman who had anticipated this was already unloading her light bulbs and laundry detergent onto the check-out counter.

An elderly woman with a cane in the cart, surrounded by a lot of towels, had surprising speed and agility. She was already ahead of me by the time I had turned my cart into the next lane. She looked ahead only, ostensibly looking at the woman in front of her, who had clearly raided the trial-size section and was no doubt preparing to take her family of six on safari in Tanzania. (Travel-sized tooth-brushes, toothpaste, deodorant, six little cans of bug spray, and enough batteries to light up the night sky for at least a month.) It took 11 minutes to get to the point where the cashier said her total was $97.84. I breathed a sigh of relief, which I stopped short in the middle of, as she brought forth from her purse a wad of coupons.

It was an actual wad. It redefined "crumpled." "I have to find them," she said. She then proceeded to make two piles, and for someone with a wad of coupons that probably could have been used by a pitching coach at spring training, she was remarkably meticulous about her piles and flattening out the coupons. There were at least two eye rolls from the cashier by the time she was done sorting. She handed the smaller pile to the cashier and then, yes, in fact, wadded up the rest and returned them to her purse.

One of the coupons didn't work. The one for detergent. And the discussion about it became, well, louder, and insistent. Eventually a manager came over and overrode the register, and the woman saved 88 cents. It was hard not to break out in song at this point.

Eventually the woman's purchases got packed into eight bags, and she began to move toward the door. The cashier was frantic. "Ma'am, you have to pay," she yelled.

The woman returned sheepishly and inserted her credit card into the reader.

But, of course, it was not accepted. She pulled out another card, her cheeks flushed, and handed it to the cashier. This card was accepted, and both the customer and I breathed a visible sigh of relief.

She confirmed that everything was in the right bag—there went 45 seconds I would never get back—and took off.

The cashier turned her attention to the elderly woman with all the towels. Senior Towel Lady had been taking her bath towels, hand towels, and washcloths out of her cart, and now she put them on the conveyor belt.

"Are these not all the same?" the cashier asked.

"Some of them, I think, are the same."

So the cashier went through 16 towels, hand towels, and wash-cloths individually. And then the woman couldn't find her purse. And then her wallet. And then she started looking around. For someone. Whom she could not see. So she fumbled a bit more, and I overheard her say, "Where is he? I'll have to use my card now."

She was looking for her husband. She didn't see him, and I heard her mutter, "Where the hell is he?" She frowned.

He eventually showed up. After she had paid with her credit card, though I expect fuming in the check-out line comes with an additional cost. She was clearly mad though she had held it together so far.

He explained that he looked for her and saw a bathroom and chose to get that out of the way. She wasn't buying it. And they were oblivious of the fact that I needed to move into the check-out, where they now stood looking at each other. He apologized many times and in different ways, but somehow with my luck, she accepted none of them.

"I couldn't see you," he said.

"You never do," she replied tartly. And their conversation went downhill from there.

The cashier finally spoke up. "Could I ask you to move? I have customers waiting."

Twenty-seven minutes after I entered the check-out line, I reached the cashier. I inserted my credit card in the reader. All went well—until the receipt got tangled up in the printer. And it had to be fixed. Right then.

It was at that moment that I realized I had forgotten ice cream. I moaned inaudibly to myself and decided to suck it up. I was not going back. I had been through too much already. I paid, put the groceries in the car, and drove home.

Maybe next time would be better. Or not.

Because I've made picking the wrong line an Olympic Sport. I'm sure to get a medal—if I can get to the finish line. The car ahead of me in my lane isn't moving. It seems to have stalled.

I felt bad for the man reading the Qur'an on the train this morning. He spent more time looking at other people than reading. It was clear that he was wondering if they were looking at him. I smiled at him several times, and he smiled nervously back. Everyone else was involved in email or social media on their phone and never even looked up. Yet this man was still the most nervous person on our end of the train. I couldn't help wondering whether someone had said or done something to him sometime in the past that caused his nervousness.

It's not every day you find yourself in the big box store at 9:50 in the evening and see a high school kid covered in bandages and blood being wheeled on a stretcher by six EMTs. And the kid had a grin on his face, loving all the attention. He was followed by an older woman who was on her cell phone.

I heard her say loudly, "I have people dying on me all the time."

It took me a minute to realize she was not related to the young man. I realized this when she asked an employee, "What time is it?" (She was still on her phone.)

"We close in 10 minutes. It's 9:50."

"Ten minutes?" the woman on the phone yelled. "I have to go. I have shopping to get done." She grabbed a grocery cart and wheeled off into the store.

The kid was nearly out the door and still grinning, talking with an EMT.

I looked at the cashier. He was probably no older than 22, maybe younger. "We got some weird stuff going on here," he said.

I started to ask him to say more, but he shook his head immediately. "You don't want to know. Really. You don't want to know. Are you saving with our discount card today?"

I wasn't. I paid and left. There were two rescue trucks still in front of the store.

I'm glad I didn't have that much drama in my life today. I hope the kid was okay. My guess is he thought he was, but whether he was or not involves a lot more than bandages. The older woman seemed lonely. I could be wrong about that, of course. But why was she talking with someone on the phone oblivious of the store closing in 10 minutes?

There's always more to a person's story. Sometimes we don't get to learn what it is. So you wish them well and hope they find a little peace and comfort. And you say thank you that your life, at the moment, isn't like that. Still, I did enjoy making up stories about those people on the way home.

PART FOUR

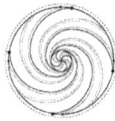

When Children
Are Present

A nine year old in my tennis class had a meltdown today. He said I was being unfair to him. I tried talking to him and then, when I could see he was determined, I let him go ahead and melt down. There was a part of me that admired his stubbornness. I sensed he knew he needed to melt down. The sobs were hard to hear, but I let him sob. I suspect he'd been bottling up some emotions for a long time. I talked with his dad later and learned this was not his first meltdown.

And then, to let all this go before my tennis match this evening, I listened to music while I was eating dinner—one song over and over, "Sweet Nothing."

I played well in my tennis match. Afterwards I said a prayer that my nine year old student would learn resiliency in his life. I hope he can find his song, whatever form it takes. Healing, after all, comes in many forms after many different kinds of hurt.

There were surprisingly long lines at the check-out today. I had only four items, but there I was. Waiting. And moving slowly.

To pass time, I smiled back at the one year old girl playing with her cotton soccer ball in the cart in front of me.

Her parents were in conversation.

She grinned and threw me the ball and squealed when I caught it.

Her parents turned and watched.

I threw the ball back in front of her and she picked it up, looked at her parents, and threw it back at me. Then she fell down and looked up with a grin.

I grinned back. I tossed her the ball, and to everyone's surprise, she caught it. She was pleased with herself, giggling and grinning at everyone.

Her parents looked at each other and told me that Maya hadn't caught anything before but a cold. (Maya is either headed for Comedy Central or a profession as a pharmacist, I'm not sure which.)

We threw the ball back and forth and she loved to chase it down, look at her folks, and then throw it to me. And then laugh. It was hard to tell who was having the better time.

The 20-minute wait in line seemed like the most fun I'd ever had standing in line. I threw the ball to Maya one last time as she stood in the cart and was wheeled away.

I told her dad that the store should pay her for making the line bearable.

He replied that he didn't want to break child labor laws or have to pay taxes on the income, so the fun was free.

But as I looked at all the people standing in line, sour expressions on their faces, looking at plastic utensils and deciding if they were worth the extra dollar, or paying rapt attention to their phones, I realized that for once I'd picked the right line.

Some days you just get lucky and can only say thank you. I did that today and can still feel the smile of a happy one year old with twinkling eyes and a joy for life. It's kept me smiling all day.

Apparently, I am scary. Coming back to my loft after a trip to the gym, in my building I rounded a corner just as a toddler came down the hall.

She looked at me, screamed, and then started crying for her mother.

I suppose it's hard to appear soothing when you have sweat dripping off of you, but I tried—to no avail.

The toddler raced into her mother's arms. Thankfully, the young mom was laughing, and she gave me a smile as she hugged her sobbing daughter. "Were you surprised by the nice man as he came around the corner?" she asked her daughter.

The child wailed more loudly.

The mom looked apologetically at me.

"Well, I won't have to spend a lot for a Halloween costume this year," I said. "All I need is seven miles on the elliptical machine."

The young mom mouthed," I'm sorry," but I waved her off.

The toddler turned and saw her mother smiling. "See, he's a nice man. He's not scary at all."

The toddler took just a second to appraise me before she started wailing again.

"I'll just go—and shower," I said, mostly to myself, since I suspected the mom couldn't hear me over the crying.

She waved a little good-bye with an endearing embarrassed look, and I raced for my place, though I did look around the two corners on the way. I didn't want to develop a reputation.

I nearly kidnapped a toddler in a store this evening. The little girl, maybe about three years old, looked at me, smiled, and yelled, "Daddy."

I smiled back and looked around for where her actual dad (or mom) was.

It turned out her dad was a 30-something year-old guy, about six feet tall and clearly in great shape. How his daughter confused us, I'll never know. But when I asked him if she did that all the time, he said she'd never done it before.

Nonetheless, she waved at me as I proceeded with my cart toward paper towels and diet iced tea.

I am bothered by what I saw a mother teaching her son today.

I was filling my car with gas and then went to replace the air freshener, which took maybe 45 seconds to do. It would have taken 30, but at about 15 seconds this woman started honking at me for not pulling away from the gas pump fast enough. I was startled, looked up, waved, and then went on replacing the air freshener.

In the grocery store today, I was pushing my cart (to get iced tea, of course) and passed a mother perusing pork chops while her two year old sat in the seat of the cart looking bored.

But then the child looked up at me, got a huge grin on her face, and said, "Dada."

The mother twirled around quickly and saw me more than a few feet away, waving back at her child.

The toddler giggled.

"That's not Dada," the mother said, but she smiled at me.

I beamed back at both of them.

When the father came up, African American like the mom and the toddler, I wondered what had caused the child's reaction. Was it our smiles that were similar, our eyes, the shape of our faces, the smell, a movement? I'll never know. I do know though that the toddler's grin and giggle have stayed with me all day.

At 12:30 a.m., a woman with three kids was next to me at the baggage claim. She was organizing the kids and their bags while I was waiting for mine. The one boy among the three, probably age 11 or so, was tired of waiting, I could tell.

As soon as I had my bags, the boy began circling me for some unknown reason. His mother fussed at him. "Shepard, watch where you are going."

He circled me, and his mother was clearly both frustrated and appalled. I was amused actually.

"Shepard, why are you circling him?"

The boy stopped finally and considered this, but had no answer.

"Maybe he's an Australian," I suggested, a grin spreading across my face.

Now the mother stopped and looked at me, and she was not connecting the dots. This stranger had said something that didn't compute for her and he could be dangerous.

I tried again. "Well, I wondered if Shepard was Australian because I feel like I'm being herded." I waited for comprehension.

She was puzzled. "Australian? Why would you think he's an Australian?" And then she did the near perfect stop. "Australian Shepard," she said in a low voice, and then she laughed.

I joined in.

Shepard was now confused by the laughter.

"Thanks," I said. I smiled at him. "Both your mom and I will be more awake till we get where we're going."

He looked toward his mother, who now had a mischievous look to her.

"I'll tell you later," she told him. She smiled.

And I added, "When you can be a good boy, sit, and enjoy a treat."

I wished them good night and I heard the woman chuckling as I headed toward the front door and the parking shuttle.

It made having a delayed flight and wet luggage totally worth it.

I was having dinner out tonight. At the next table was an African American grandmother with her three girls, somewhere between the ages of four and nine, I'd guess. The grandmother was doing her best to teach manners, with some success though I suspect everyone was tired.

"Don't use your fingers." "Hold your fork like this." "Use a napkin." "Please take your sister to the rest room while I clean up Tanya's face."

The four year old kept looking at me with her messy face, smiling and waving.

I smiled and waved back.

The other girls, when they returned from the rest room, looked to see who had the youngest's attention.

I smiled back at them.

The grandmother gave me a look and apologized. "I hope they aren't bothering you, sir," she said.

"Not in the slightest," I replied. "They made me smile. I've been worried for our country. And it will be our children who can give us hope that things will get better."

The grandmother gave me a look and then said quietly, "Thank you."

"Thank them," I said. "And thank you for teaching them to be kind."

PART FIVE

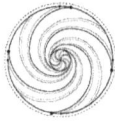

Wondering, Remembering, Grieving, Praying

There was lots of last-minute Christmas shopping today. I asked one cashier if she was surviving.

She said, "I've been here 10 hours already. Some child asked me why we were out of a toy I'd never heard of and then started to cry when I didn't know. To make matters worse, I thought his mom was going to hit him."

She saw me starting to smile. "No," she continued. "She had her hand raised, but she stopped since I was looking at her."

"Thank you for looking at her," I said.

She nodded slowly at my response.

"I hope the day gets better," I added.

"Me too." She sighed.

Here's a prayer of peace and love for all of those folks frazzled by the holidays. May we be kind to the people working through everyone's anxiety. They take on a lot.

Safe at home tonight. On a day when millions marched for women's rights and equality across the planet, I sat on a plane next to a woman whose husband insisted they sit next to me in the exit row even though the plane was half empty and there were some completely empty rows. He wanted to stretch his legs forward. Then he insisted she move from the window seat and sit next to me because he wanted to sit next to the wall.

She tried to talk to him. No luck. Their son, who was sitting behind us, tried to talk to him. No luck. The son gave up, rolling his eyes at me.

The dad suggested I could move if I wanted more room, which created a dilemma for me. I didn't want to give in to his stubbornness, but I felt badly for his wife.

"I was here first," I said, as pleasantly as possible. "If you want more space, you're free to move."

They didn't. Until thankfully the son came up after the seat belt sign went off and invited his mother to come talk to him. She nearly sprinted away with great relief on her face. On a day when so many people found some hope through public action, I wished this woman had gotten some of that feeling too. And maybe she did from her son.

Interestingly enough, her husband kind of sulked after she left. He sat there and rifled through the airline magazine. There was nothing he really needed his wife for at the moment though he did get the flight attendant to fetch things for him. "I need cream," he said, even though the flight attendant had asked earlier and he had not responded.

I hope his wife's life isn't like that every day, and I hope he finds some joy in their relationship that doesn't require his demanding his way. These few minutes with these people also made me think about all the people who have harder lives than this woman. I pray for a world where we treat each other with decency and respect. And I give thanks to all of my friends who were out there marching today for women's rights and equality.

I'm thinking about an older woman I saw today walking by the condiments who saw me turn into her aisle. She stopped in order not to hit my cart. Her husband ran into her with his cart. She apologized to him and me. I apologized to her. Her husband just glared. At her. And never apologized for hitting her with the cart. As they rounded the corner, she was still apologizing while he was still clearly angry.

Was this the story of her life? While there are a number of possible scenarios, I still wonder if it was. For her sake (and his), I hope not.

Walking from South Station to my office this morning, I encountered a man that I was pretty sure was homeless, with a cat on a leash. The cat clearly didn't want to be on the leash. But it was easy to see how much the man wanted the cat near him. I found myself hoping he would be able to keep the cat at least for a while, and that he could care for the cat while the cat was there for him. I wondered what his stories were—how he ended up homeless, with the cat, how he found the cat. I also wondered how the stories would play out. I hope he treats the cat well.

It was a moment for thoughts and questions—no moral for me, just a sign of our world today, and our desire to be loved, have companionship, have a purpose. And to survive. I hope they both do—and with each other.

My friend Deborah and her husband Gene have lived in the same house in the same fairly affluent Maryland neighborhood for about 20 years. I know Deborah through our mutual trainings on the Enneagram. Gene, a medical doctor with an excellent reputation, is a man of routine. Most mornings he runs the same route to the gym to work out. This morning on his run, he was pulled over by two police cars, made to lie down on the ground, and handcuffed.

I live in a neighborhood with a significantly higher crime rate than the neighborhood where Deborah and Gene live. I go out walking a lot in my neighborhood. I've never once been pulled over or questioned by the police. I head out of my building in tennis shorts a lot, and I have never been handcuffed.

Thankfully, Gene was not physically hurt. But no jogger, regardless of race, should have to endure that. I have no doubts though that if my skin were darker, at least once in my life, regardless of where I lived, I would have had Gene's experience too. And quite possibly more than once.

Deb told me tonight that she wants to see a world where this doesn't happen to her grandchildren. A world where anyone can jog and not be pulled over, put face down on the street, and handcuffed.

We don't live in that world yet. We still live in a world where there are double standards. And I can't help but think we perpetuate the problem if we pretend there aren't.

My prayer tonight is not only for Gene and Deb, but for the next jogger who gets pulled over, made to lie face down on the road, and handcuffed—and the next jogger and the next. My prayer is that we all do what we can so that those numbers get smaller and smaller until this happens no more. Deb, I'm sorry we live in a country where you fear for your grandchildren. I promise to keep working for a country where there is no longer any reason for that fear.

I'm thinking tonight of a certain Jewish child whose Hebrew baby-naming ceremony was on this October day in 2018. That child will never forget that the day that was supposed to be a private occasion was interrupted by an anti-Semitic shooter who took 11 lives and injured six other people. The child's life was changed today but not in the way anyone but the shooter hoped.

I'm thinking of all the people at that ceremony who now live with questions that begin, "What if …?" and "Why …?"

I'm thinking of the family members of the 11 who died. All their lives changed today because of hatred.

I'm thinking of the families of the two African Americans killed in Kentucky this week by a white gunman who walked into a grocery store and shot a grandfather and then went outside and shot a woman and is reported to have said, "Whites don't shoot whites."

I'm thinking of the child who will never see his grandfather again.

I'm thinking of the African American church and the people who were inside when the Kentucky gunman tried to enter but could not. I'm thinking of the questions and fears they now live with.

I'm thinking of those affected by this week's events, people who believe their houses of worship should be safe.

I remember the victims and survivors of First Baptist Church in Sutherland, Texas.

I remember the victims and survivors of Emanuel AME Church in Charleston, South Carolina, who were shot by the white supremacist.

I remember the victims and survivors of the shooting at the Tennessee Valley Unitarian Universalist Church 10 years ago during a worship service where children were front and center. One man gave his life so that more would be spared.

I remember all religious people who have died or been terrorized by violence in their places of worship.

I hold close all of those who were traumatized and re-traumatized by these latest acts of terrorism.

I pray for a better world, one with less violence, fewer threats of violence, less hatred, and more respect and love.

I pray we never forget the people we've lost, the people who lost someone they loved, the people who were terrorized and traumatized by these violent acts.

I pray this violence will end.

I pray each of us does one act that promotes kindness, respect, and peace to those around us.

I pray each of us reaches out to others with more love.

I spent time today wondering if I could ever shoot someone's child and believe I had a justifiable reason to do that. I also spent today thinking about parents of color having to teach their children how to keep from being shot, and wondering how many white mothers teach their children such lessons.

On October 6, 1998, 20 years ago today, Matthew Shepard was left for dead tied to a fence in Laramie, Wyoming. He was 21. He died six days later. I was working that weekend with our congregation in Golden, Colorado, two hours south of Laramie. The following weekend on behalf of Unitarian Universalism, at the request of our congregations in Cheyenne and Laramie and Casper, I returned to represent our faith in an interfaith event in Cheyenne. I was one of only a handful of clergy willing to be there.

Fred Phelps and a contingent from Westboro Baptist Church were due to show up and protest the event. (They apparently did show up later that week though not that day.)

I was one of two ministers willing to be filmed for local TV news. It was a day when a lot of people in our country needed hope.

The next day I spoke to our congregation in Laramie and then accompanied people from the area to visit the fence where Matthew had been left to die.

Later that night I visited some people in Casper to help them try to comprehend how such a thing could happen. I still remember the young man who could say only, "Matthew was my friend," before he ran out of words, trying but failing to hold back tears.

Matthew would be 41 today. Dennis Shepard, Matthew's father, told the killers when they were found guilty that he did not want them to die. He wanted them to remember that they had life every day they were alive and that Matthew did not.

Four years ago this month, 17 year old Laquon McDonald, an African American youth, was shot 16 times by a police officer who was initially cleared of wrongdoing until video showed Laquon walking away from the officer when he was shot and fell to the ground. The video showed Laquon being shot 15 more times in about 15 seconds. Today, the officer was found guilty of second degree murder and 16 counts of aggravated assault. The officer could have been found guilty of first degree murder, but the jury felt fear was the cause of the murder, though they did feel the fear was unreasonable. There are about 1,000 police shootings a year in this country. African American men are three times more likely to die from police action than white men.

One in three women will be the victim of sexual violence this year. Only 9% of the victims of sexual assault are men. Only 37% of sexual assaults are reported to the authorities. One in four girls and one in six boys will be the victims of sexual assault. Of the people who abuse children, 96% are male. Only 12% of child sexual abuse cases are reported to the authorities.

These last two weeks many victims of sexual assault were triggered again as a woman publicly reported a sexual assault. Because of Dr. Christine Ford's testimony at the U.S. Supreme Court confirmation hearing for Justice Brett Kavanagh, many women have now publicly told their own stories of sexual assault.

They listened to Dr. Ford's testimony and then watched Senator Lindsay Graham yell at Senator Dianne Feinstein. They listened as pundits said that was the moment that rallied Republicans in the Senate. They watched a Supreme Court nominee yell angrily at the Democrats (three women and five men) about the way he was being treated. Sexual assault victims listened as the president of the United States ridiculed Dr. Ford at a rally earlier this week, mocking her testimony.

Victims of sexual assault do not have the privilege to mock their attackers. Their stories, their lives, have been forever changed by the assault. Their chances for justice are slim.

Those who have died no longer have a story.

I've spent 20 years thinking of what Matthew Shepherd's story might have gone on to include. I think of every young African American man, every child of color, whose parents teach them now how to stay alive and who pray to keep them alive because what they teach is not enough. I think of every victim of sexual assault whose life is changed every time another assault makes news, is downplayed, questioned, and mocked.

I pray for a country where each person can tell the multiplicity of their stories, where people are respected for these stories, where people can say what they are for and be heard. I pray for a country free from oppression, free from our history of double standards, power over, and violence toward others.

I pray for a country where people can live without the fear of being held down, assaulted, laughed at, tied up, shot 16 times, and killed.

I pray for a country where we ask questions of ourselves instead of pointing fingers at others.

In these last 20 years, when schools and churches have been places where people go to end the lives of others with an automatic rifle, when we have pretended that not so many women and children have been sexually assaulted, when a person of color cannot risk seeing the police as their protectors rather than as their potential killers, I pray for a country that is less violent than the one we live in at this moment and have lived in these last 20 Octobers.

I pray for the end of violence. I pray for the lives of those forever altered or lost.

I pray for a better country.

I pray I can be better.

I pray we can better.

I pray we do more than pray.

I pray that our children find hope and make a better country for their children.

Today, on this day of yet another mass shooting in this country, and forever I grieve the loss of life. I grieve for the people who died in every mass shooting. I grieve for their families, friends, and co-workers. I grieve for those who were there and feel both lucky and guilty that they survived while others died.

I grieve for those who are reminded of their own losses. The parents and family. The church members. All those who know someone who has been lost in a mass shooting and feel the rise of emotion when another one happens.

I grieve for those who have died and those who loved them who died when we did not pay attention. Having served as a chaplain at San Francisco General Hospital, and having been trained as a Hospice Volunteer during the AIDS epidemic, I watched many people die whether they were homeless or gay or people of color and no one really noticed.

I grieve for police officers and safety officials who are trained in how to respond to mass shootings.

I grieve for workers who must look at and remove the bodies, who try and keep the wounded alive, who must tell family members that someone they loved has died or been hurt.

I grieve for the first responders who will never forget the day.

I grieve for the reporters trying to tell a story while witnessing and listening to horrific details.

I grieve for the parents who must explain what happened to their children.

I grieve for parents who have wondered if they should have done more when they've seen hatred and anger come from their children.

I grieve for the parents who simply turned away or encouraged the hatred and anger. I grieve for the parents who say they didn't see this coming from their children.

I grieve for schools that do not have the resources to educate and manage children, where they know some children will slip through the cracks.

I grieve for those who believe there are sides and lines to be drawn.

There are no sides. We all lose. We only move forward by laying down our own sword of words and being with one another, seeing each other's humanity, and reminding ourselves that the responsibility to be a human being means remembering we are one human among billions of people on a planet.

I grieve for a planet full of people who forget that a leading tenet of every major religion in the world is to treat others as you would like to be treated.

I grieve for those who will be assumed to be bad people because they are perceived to be like a shooter—because they are Muslim, because they live with mental health issues, because they own a gun, or because they happen to share some other coincidental identification.

I grieve for our country when we rush to believe that only others have responsibility for a shooting. We must come together for the sake of each other.

I grieve for those who will die and those who will lose loved ones in the next shooting.

And the next.

And the next.

And the next.

And the next.

Until we decide they must stop.

Until we act.

I grieve for a country and for a planet where this violence is all too common, all too familiar.

I pray that each of us commits to be a little more humane, a little more compassionate, a little more willing to come together with others to be a part of solution.

I pray that we work together to end hatred and superiority.

I pray that we decide to become better people today.

I pray we never forget.

I pledge to remember.

I pledge to become a better person.

I pledge to be a part of the solution, however many solutions it takes.

PART SIX

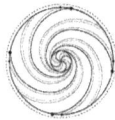

What Really Matters

What Really Matters

At baggage claim in the Minneapolis airport, I was approached by a young woman who was clearly trying to cope with being new in this country. She told me she was from Somalia, and she said in halting English that she did not know where to go to get picked up outside. It took a couple of minutes and several repeated questions for me to figure out exactly what she was saying—that she would text someone to pick her up.

She started to go in the right direction, juggling three bags. Then she saw someone with a luggage cart and indicated to me that that was what she wanted. I pointed to where they were.

She wanted to put a $20 bill into the slot, but the machine only took singles and fives.

I explained this to her about three times, and then she suddenly understood. "Do they take card?" she asked, pulling out a debit card. I nodded yes, but she couldn't figure out that you have to insert the card and pull it back out quickly, so I did it for her. And then I helped her load up the cart.

I pointed to a door to the outside and she nodded. But once I had my luggage collected, she started to follow me. However, I was heading to the rental cars. I tried to explain, and I think she at last understood that she ought not to follow me. I pointed to the door, and she nodded and headed that way.

Before I left, I stopped to watch, marveling at this young woman and her courage to be here, showing up at the airport with no one meeting her, and not knowing what to do. I felt honored that she found me approachable. As she headed out the door, I said a prayer of hope and care for her and her new life.

When I got to my rental car and left the garage, I saw her outside the terminal on a bench, texting like a world-class pro, and perhaps she was, though surely in another language. My fear for her lessened as I glimpsed a smile on her face, and I hoped she was on her way to good things and would be welcomed here by those she met. I marveled at what she was doing.

Dad was worried. He'd heard that Friday night was the second busiest flight day for Orlando. I was pretty sure that was for inbound flights. But my sister dropped me off early anyway for my outbound flight.

Sure enough, most of the cars heading into the airport were headed toward Arrivals, not Departures.

I breezed through bag check and headed toward security, where there was only a woman with a little boy ahead of me. I heard sobbing. The boy was scared. But it was the mother who was sobbing.

The TSA agent tried a couple of times to assure her everything would be all right, and finally she began to settle down. She headed toward the scanners after having her boarding pass checked.

When I stepped up to the podium, I asked the agent if the woman was okay.

"Nervous flyer," the agent said. "We've all been there unless we're A-List like you." I smiled. And she sent me through.

I got in line behind the anxious woman, who was still anxious but better. Her child, maybe about four years old, seemed less afraid.

I loaded my computer, tablet, wallet, belt, and phone into three different trays. I walked through the scanner. Once through, I saw my trays at the end of the belt.

And then I saw the mom, desperately looking around. "I don't see my bag," she said frantically. She looked at the other conveyer belt and didn't see it there either. She looked around wildly and eventually found a TSA agent. She told him she couldn't find her bag.

The agent looked at her, then at the boy, and then shrugged. This irked me.

I collected my things and approached the woman. I said, "Perhaps they had to re-scan it. Let's see if it comes through again."

She looked at me, panicked. I told her I flew all the time and this had happened to me.

She nodded slowly, then went back to looking frantically for her bag.

A moment later another TSA agent appeared at the side of the conveyor belt, holding a bag. "Whose is this?" he asked.

She said quickly, "Mine."

"I have to go through it," he said. She nodded and approached his station.

He opened her bag and found the culprit immediately. An apple juice bottle. He told her he had to confiscate it, and she winced. Then she nodded.

He ran the bag again, leaving her and her son alone. I told her, "I do that way too often."

"Mommy's just having a bad day," she said, as much to me as to her son.

I nodded as the agent handed her the apple-juiceless bag. "What airline?" I asked.

She told me the gate and the airline, and that they were headed to her mother's new home in Texas for Christmas.

I pointed her in the right direction, and even though it wasn't my direction, I told her to follow me. She scooped up her bag and took her little boy by the hand. He seemed happier now.

I walked with them till we could see the gate number. Her body relaxed. She turned to me and smiled. "Thank you," she said.

I smiled back and wished her a Merry Christmas. I waved at the little guy, who smiled and waved back.

"Let me give you something for your trouble," the woman said, again slightly anxious.

I held up my hand and refused. "Give it to Santa." I smiled.

She nodded and we waved again. I turned back down the hall.

Normally I hate arriving too early for my flight. But this was not one of those days.

I went to the grocery store tonight for milk and bacon and de-caf coffee. I followed a scruffy looking guy, white, maybe about 40 years old, into the store. As I walked to the far back corner where the milk was, I noticed he had stopped at the magazines and was looking intently at the bottom shelf. I didn't think much of it until I walked back on the way to bacon and coffee. Then I noticed him examining the leftover Christmas wrapping paper and decorations. And after I got my coffee and bacon, I noticed him, empty-handed, looking at school supplies.

Was he there getting warm? Did he not like the selections? Had I just caught him at odd moments in the store so that his behavior struck me as out of place? Was he shoplifting? Maybe he had to get out of the house for a bit because someone at home was drinking too much or driving him crazy. I'll never know.

Had he been an African American teenager, would I have thought about his behavior differently? Had it been a mother with a kid in a shopping cart, would I have thought about it differently?

Politicians in our over-simplified world spend a lot of time reducing people to a single story. In an accelerated world, all of us may need to simplify somewhat in order to cope. But often that means simplifying the other person, eventually to a one-dimensional version. I started thinking about how this scruffy guy had to be a collection of stories—stories that I will never know even though I could easily have reduced him to one story. I'm not even sure what that story would have been. It seems to me, particularly when many people are hardening their rhetoric and more dangerously their opinions and judgments, that we desperately need to see others as more than a single story.

I'm afraid most of us don't notice the guy in the store, or we notice and then immediately write him off by attributing to him the one story that comes first to mind. But everyone we pass is a collection of stories we know nothing about. And if we don't realize that about others, why should we ask others to recognize that about us?

My hope and prayer is that we intentionally slow down and not reduce the people we encounter to a single story but acknowledge that they embody many stories that we will never know.

Tonight I mainly hope that the guy at the grocery store found what he needed there, whatever it was—warmth, refuge, breath mints, a spatula, or *National Geographic*. And I hope too that no one else there attempted to reduce him to a single story and that someone else besides me took some time to wonder what his stories are.

My friend Scott, whom I knew before seminary, messaged me recently about a book. I ordered a used copy, and I pulled it out of the mailbox today. So this evening I sat down to read it, and I was inundated by memories.

The book is about one remarkable place. A hospital. The only public hospital in San Francisco. The hospital that takes every patient, regardless, and cares for them. Cares for them until they leave. Or cares for them until they die.

My first semester of seminary, back in Berkeley in 1993, was an eye-opener to be sure. I was just 32, and living further away from home than I had in my entire life. I had never lived in a metropolitan area of 8,000,000 people, never lived without a car, never lived in such diversity.

I was taking classes on ethics, theology, spirituality, church history, social justice, church administration and leadership, and a very intense class on death and dying, which would become the foundation for all my learning throughout seminary. The class was taught by a Holocaust survivor, a Jewish chaplain whose specialty was as a suicidologist. We were asked to pair up with another student, and my new friend Barbara and I did that, having dinner after each class to talk through what we were learning and experiencing. It was the beginning of a lifelong friendship.

My friend Scott was doing his hospital chaplaincy that semester at San Francisco General Hospital. In October, a little over a month after I had started seminary, Scott asked me if I had any interest in doing my hospital chaplaincy there after the beginning of the new year because a prospective student chaplain had dropped out. It took me two seconds to say I was interested, even though I had no idea what I was getting myself into. Scott arranged for me to come visit the hospital to meet the chaplain leaders, an Episcopal priest and a Baptist minister. I would get a tour to see if I could handle it.

So I went with Scott to the hospital. I was introduced to the chaplains, who took me immediately to the same setting where the book I now have is set—the AIDS ward. If I could handle this, they said, I was probably going to be okay as a chaplain.

I remember stepping off the elevator, not knowing what to expect. I had done hospice training in my home town, Lexington, Kentucky, so I could volunteer, and I had also taught a child with HIV after school there. I was grateful for both experiences, so none of what I was now seeing seemed particularly new or frightening. Ward 5A seemed like it could be in any hospital, with staff bustling about and people in beds. Assured somewhat by the fact that I didn't freak out, they offered me a chaplain's position, even though I was a new seminarian. I would start in January. And even though I would watch Scott come back from the hospital always looking overwhelmed, I was hopeful and eager.

In the death and dying class, we'd had a role-play that had been tremendously powerful and at the time controversial. A student was asked to play the role of the chaplain visiting a patient in the hospital. The student chaplain in the role-play, a very kind and sweet-hearted man, was admonished for taking the hand of the patient. He was stunned, and so were the rest of us. But the teacher said to us, "The patient feels out of control. They may not want to hold your hand. By your taking it without them asking, you are making them feel more out of control. If they ask to be touched, you can touch them. But give the patient some dignity and control over their body. It might be the only time they have that." I carried that lesson into my first day, unsure of what to expect. But it had been a powerful lesson.

I met my fellow chaplain students. Bruce was a Catholic priest, about five feet tall, who introduced himself with a laugh and a joke. "You should know I'm the one straight priest in San Francisco." We all knew he wasn't the only one, but it was a curious introduction. Joyce was a Lutheran pastor on sabbatical from her ministry in North Carolina. She was visiting a friend and doing a "different kind of ministry" than in her small rural church. She was loving being in a city, though she refused to ride the subway as she was sure she'd be underneath the Bay and drowned when "the earthquake" hit. Juana was a lay pastor in her Baptist church, a tall, soft-spoken woman who had to remind everyone she was from Panama and was not African American, even though her skin color was very dark. Bertha was accepted into the program because her son worked as a nurse at the hospital. She came from a Primitive Baptist church in Maryland and told us that in the eyes of many back home, it was "scandalous" for her to be working in this program.

We spent the first day in orientation. I still wasn't quite sure what I had signed up for but I headed back for day two on a Wednesday. With only about 15 minutes of preparation and training, we were turned loose to go be chaplains and visit patients. This was something I would do for five months—in what would likely become the best practical hands-on education ever.

Because I needed a certain number of credit hours, I was assigned to three other wards—pediatrics (because of my teaching background), the ward where there were people who had broken bones (mainly due to alcohol-related accidents), and the psych ward. I did also get to visit the prison ward, where I was escorted in and out by police, and I had two weekend rotations in the emergency room.

The emergency room was the place where humility had seeped into the walls. You couldn't walk in there and not wonder how many people over the span of a decade had come through, clung to life, and died here. The only place where the San Francisco's homeless and poor population could get medical attention. The place where the forgotten were treated with humanity and care.

I saw a homeless man come into the cafeteria one day at lunch, wild eyed. As Bob, my supervisor, got up to take his tray back, the homeless man took it and sat down to finish the meal of uneaten scraps. When Bob offered to buy him his own meal instead, the man shook his head, stood up, and took the pork chop bone with him as he sped out.

I visited a man on the psych ward who asked me to go get his pile of clothes, which he said were on a street corner in the Mission District, as he wanted to change. For five visits in a row, we would repeat the conversation where I would listen, he would realize I wouldn't yell or hurt him, that he could potentially trust me, and then he would ask me to get his clothes. He never remembered that we'd had this conversation two days before. He eventually died, never having had a visitor. The hospital was never quite sure of his identity.

I talked with a Russian immigrant who had purposely infected himself with HIV through shared needles so someone would pay attention to him and he could get some care for his health. I remember the prisoner who asked for a Bible, desperately asking me to tell the officers he was getting his life turned around, and could I speak on his behalf? I remember the many, many people who came into the AIDS ward and died there, sometimes with people around them, sometimes not.

Two cases always stood out to me. One was a child of about six on the pediatric ward. He had two broken arms and a broken leg. And he was now alone. His mother had died. She had committed suicide by jumping off the Bridge. (Even though there are multiple bridges in the San Francisco Bay Area, the Golden Gate Bridge was the "Suicide Bridge" or simply "the Bridge" to those in the hospital.)

The child's mother hadn't wanted to die alone. So she jumped with her son in her arms. Her body cushioned the blow when they hit the water, enough so that only she lost her life. I would occasionally read the boy a story, though mostly, I just came into the room and played with things, so that he might play with things—and I'd color. The art therapist and I watched his pictures—fiery reds and oranges that she said expressed his anger in a way that he couldn't verbally articulate. I learned before I left that the art and play therapists had gotten him to verbalize what had happened that night on the bridge, and how life-saving it was that he could say it out loud and have it be real. I've often wondered what happened to him. He'd be in his 30's if he is still alive. Somehow as a six year old, all alone, he was given a chance.

Then there was Harold. He was in and out of critical care when I first met him. I was asked to go and talk to his partner, the lead chaplain said, though the nurse referred to the partner only as his friend. When I went to the unit, Harold was strapped to what seemed like every machine possible.

In short, Harold had no hope. The nurse told me when his friend would stop by and ask if I could come back. His friend would be the one who needed someone to talk to. They were going to ask his friend to agree to take him off life support. He had no chance. His father, a minister, and a police officer from Missouri had come out and then given up on him too, convinced he was going to die.

Yet his partner, his friend, believed he did have a chance. He knew Harold was a fighter. We talked for weeks, and eventually when the doctors and nurses met with him to ask him if they could turn off the machines, I was asked by the man to be there with him when he told them no. No one was happy. But Harold's friend, his partner, visited every day after work and talked to him. And about two weeks after the unhappy meeting, Harold woke up. No one quite knew why or how. I still remember him wiggling his finger at me, very slowly one day when his partner introduced me as the man who'd shown up and just listened.

I watched Harold move from wiggling a finger to eating on his own, sitting up, taking a step, eventually walking out on his own from the hospital. I never saw them again. I have wondered how long he lived, if he is still alive—he'd be around 55 now—and if he is still with his partner.

So on Easter, when I think about the meaning of the resurrection story, I always think of San Francisco General Hospital. The refuge that gave life back to so many people. And two powerful resurrection stories that remind me that the power to be a presence in the life of others, the ability to give hope and to companion people in their life, is perhaps the greatest gift of all. I think what I learned from San Francisco General is that you can't change people, you can't always even touch people, but you can bear witness. Every time I think of San Francisco General, I remember those who died. Those who cared. And those who experienced a resurrection back into living more fully, sometimes as they died, sometimes as they got better. Remembering and being present to these stories makes my life less painful. These stories give me new life too.

One of the messages I got from watching "Star Trek Beyond" today (and I'm not giving the movie away here) is this: Alone, we are our own worst enemy. I thought about it most of the day.

It began to change at dinner when it turned into: Alone, I can be a restaurant's worst enemy. I went to this restaurant for dinner and was seated, and then ignored for 15 minutes. Finally, I got up and left after the third server passed me without comment.

The hostess saw me as I approached the door. "Is something wrong, sir?"

"No server ever stopped by."

"Why didn't you use the order screen or signal someone?" (Where's the "I'm sorry" piece of her customer service training?) They weren't busy either.

"I'll just go somewhere else. To see whether it's me or you."

No response, but I was almost out the door.

And I did get better service at the restaurant next door, where I left the server a 30% tip—even though she messed up the check. (She apologized and fixed it immediately.)

Later, I wrote to the first restaurant's website a note about my experience. I told them I won't boycott them (though it might be a while before I go back to that particular restaurant), but that the experience did leave an impression—most especially the question about why I didn't order on the machine at my table.

I added that I was glad I got to see the beginning of a happy expression on the server's face at the restaurant next door when she saw the size of the tip, despite having messed up the check. The thing is she was kind, so I was kind in return. In the end, I think that's what matters.

I woke up this morning to a very wet carpet between my bathroom and my bedroom, right outside the water heater closet. Sure enough, the floor was soaked. I let the maintenance office know. They came immediately, did as thorough an inspection as they could, and decided the first best guess would be caulking between the closet and the bathroom shower. So John caulked it, ran the wet vac on the carpet, and soaked up all the water in the closet. He let me know after an hour's work, not even stopping for the glass of water I offered him, that if something else happened, I should go and find him. But he thought the job was really done. He showed me the caulk job and explained why he thought this was right, but he wasn't sure because the water heater obstructed the view in the closet.

I went on about my day with phone calls, email, and research, and then when I went back to the area, I stepped on a wet carpet. I went to the office and let Danielle, the property manager, know it was happening again, and she went immediately to find John, who showed up with a selfie stick and his phone and tried to make a video around the heater to see if he could tell what was going on. He went not only to the loft above me (where apparently the doctor who lives there keeps his air conditioning going at 65 even when he's not there), but also to the loft two floors above me.

After 45 minutes of checking things out, John went to the office and talked with Danielle. She sent me an apologetic email and said folks would be out on Monday between 10:00 and noon to remove the water heater to see if they could find the leak. John came back, ran the wet vac again, built a bit of a dam with a board to keep the water from escaping the closet and getting onto the carpet, and told me everything Danielle had put in the email in an equally apologetic tone.

John then left me the wet vac and his cell phone number, saying if it got worse to call him over the weekend and he would come immediately. He said he didn't want anything to happen to my books, and he asked if I'm a teacher. When I told him I'm a minister, he said, "Really?" I told him I used to be a teacher and taught classes on children's literature. He thought about this but then went back to apologizing.

Then there was my visit to the grocery store this evening. There were only two cashiers and I decided, given the lines, to use the self-checkout, where there was only one person ahead of me, with only three items.

I ran everything through the scanner, but when I got to my last item, two apples, I accidentally put them on the scale before keying in the code. The sign erupted and announced to everyone nearby, "Please wait. Assistance is on the way. Someone will be with you shortly."

Except assistance wasn't on the way. The announcement, I'm happy to say, stopped its inglorious one-note song after the 10th refrain and then just flashed like a 1980 disco ball, though it felt more like "Taps" than Donna Summer or KC and the Sunshine Band. I suspect it stopped after the 10th refrain because it was tired of the customer thinking it was a liar. No help was coming.

Two young men gathering baskets strolled by without so much as a glance.

The closest cashier, who was trying to navigate among all the shoppers, flashed her eyes in my direction to acknowledge at least that I had been there a long time. Maybe she thought by now I needed a shave. She looked toward the customer service desk, which was service-less.

I considered my options. I could just walk out in a huff, leaving $65 worth of groceries on the belt, but that would seem like a complete loss. I could go find someone, but should I leave my groceries there? Would anyone take them? I could start yelling something like, "I need new blueberries because mine have gone bad since I've been in line for so long," or even "Help," but I didn't. Truly that's not the sort of person I want to be—or the sort of world I want to live in.

Finally, after 10 minutes, a young woman appeared, and the neighboring cashier three counters down pointed frantically in my direction. The young woman ambled over, mumbled an apology, and got to work.

When I let her know I'd been standing there for 10 minutes, she mumbled another apology and then created a distance between us as if I were going to make a scene and start yelling. Perhaps she had been yelled at before, but, truly, I'm much better at glaring than yelling.

Not that she offered even to bag the groceries for me, but a little bit of effort would have gone a long way. I suppose once she cleared the two apples, that would have been the moment for me to walk off in a huff, but I didn't think that quickly.

I bagged my groceries, fuming, and headed out, past a still empty customer service desk.

I couldn't help thinking about all this as I was driving home. I had a wet carpet and water all over the floor, something that hadn't really changed since morning, except that I did now have a wet vac and our maintenance man's cell phone number. Yet I felt cared for, and so I could deal with the situation.

I had all the groceries I wanted, but I never wanted to go back to that grocery store again, though I might go back there just to find a manager and describe what had happened to me.

I sent my rental property manager a note this evening saying how thankful I was that John showed up, tried to fix my leak twice, and then went the extra mile. Even though he didn't make things worse, he apologized and kept at the job.

In a world of quick fixes and quick apologies without anything more, I wonder if this is the best we can do. Or do we remember the moments when something couldn't be solved but someone did show up and showed through action or words that we mattered anyway?

We've all harmed people and done far worse things than making someone wait 10 minutes to get their apples. And yet how often do we acknowledge this and then go an extra mile?

The eighth and ninth steps for addicts in recovery are to acknowledge the harm they've done and make amends. I think if we are to recover as a people, we have to be willing to do that with respect to those we have harmed, and more besides.

We must also strive to be like John, and that may be harder. We're so pressed for time.

But if we don't take a little time for one another, then how will our time be spent? Perhaps in regressing, which is what it seems a lot of people these days are doing. Maybe we just need to try to see ourselves as being on a journey together. It won't solve everything, but I bet it would nourish our own soul as well as the souls of those accompanying us on the journey.

When I went shopping tonight, the shortest check-out line was the self-checkout. I remembered that I needed cash to tip Housekeeping at my hotel, so I got $40 back. I bagged my supplies, grabbed my receipt, and headed for the electronic door.

Only to be stopped by yelling.

The woman monitoring all the self-checkout lines was yelling, "Hey, Mister," and running toward me.

When I turned around, I saw that she wasn't just waving. It took me a moment to notice that she had my $40 in her hand. She came to a full stop in front me, catching her breath as she handed me the $40.

I must have been giving her a sheepish look because she smiled. "You're the third person tonight to do this."

I laughed, relieved and grateful. "Thank you," I said. I offered her a handshake, which she took and leaned slightly forward. I gave her a hug, barely touching her at all, given that she had to be 30 years younger than me and I didn't know her. Still, she gave me a quick hug back and smiled. "You're welcome," she said before heading back to her register.

It's amazing how one moment can have such a positive effect on your day.

I'm guessing the woman had Alzheimer's or Parkinson's. She never spoke. But she did hang on to her husband's arm—though I suppose he could have been her brother—and he never left her side.

At the restaurant at lunch I watched a server talking to the man while the woman stood there. "I'm sorry. We didn't know you were coming in," the server said apologetically to the man.

He smiled and said, "We did fine."

"Are you coming in next Saturday?" the server continued.

"I think so."

"Around 11:30?" The server looked hopeful.

The man nodded. "We'll try."

"Well, I'll remember to tell the hostess not to give away your table by the window. She's new," the server explained. "She doesn't know you yet. But I'm always glad to see you." She smiled broadly and hopefully,

The man returned the smile, as did the woman, her first change of facial expression that I observed.

"You just come back next week," the server pressed. "We'll take care of you."

"It helps when we can get out," the man said, "even though we move slowly."

"You just keep coming back." The server smiled. "You have a good week and we'll see you next Saturday."

The man waved and the two guests slowly shuffled off, arm in arm, until they were out of sight.

The server looked at me. "I forgot to refill your iced tea," she said.

"It's okay. That mattered more."

She bustled off to get my iced tea, after she'd smiled at me for a second. She returned with the tea and another apology.

"Don't worry about it all. Thank you for paying attention to what really matters."

I love watching the Olympics, but sometimes I think we should give out gold medals for something other than sports.

Today at the bus stop for long-term parking, I was joined by an elderly woman who'd been wheeled over from Baggage. It was chilly but not as cold as it had been. The bus pulled up, and I motioned for her to get on first.

Her escort helped her up, and she stepped forward and stumbled. She was going to fall. Both the escort and I leaped and caught her just in time. Thankfully, she didn't fall.

She boarded the bus, and I got my baggage loaded. We were the only two passengers. She looked at me and thanked me for keeping her from falling. I told her I had worried about her.

She told me she'd just gotten back from her son's place in Tucson and was glad to have missed the cold weather. He'd been in the Army and was now one of the few African American scientists in Tucson. He liked it there but he complained about the heat.

"Their summer is our winter," I said. I told her I had been there just a month before and I loved the mountains. She did too. We laughed about her son buying a tarp at the Army/Navy store to keep the sun out and keep his place cool since he didn't yet have air conditioning, and how that had helped.

When we got to the lot, she couldn't remember exactly where she'd parked and asked me how I remembered. I told her I wrote it down, but this time I'd parked in the same section as at Christmas where when I returned at 3:00 a.m., my car wouldn't start. I told her the location was vividly etched in my mind as a result. She laughed.

Then she remembered where her car was, and even though we were at my car, I suggested to the driver that we get her to her car first. Sure enough, her car was surrounded by snow. So we helped her out with her bag and I held her hand as she got in.

She thanked me again, and I told her that I hoped when I was her age I would be as active as she was and that people would stop and help me so I could keep being active. She smiled. And so did I.

The driver and I used our feet to get some snow out from under her tires and then we got back in the van.

It was nice to be reminded of what really matters, and to have a moment to just be there and reflect on it. I wanted to be sure to remember not so much that the escort and I kept the woman from falling, but that this encounter gave us a chance just to talk to each other like our lives mattered a little more deeply than usual.

Also, I hoped the woman would get to spend more time with her son.

My new laptop was supposed to be ready today. The IT office was taking all my stuff off my old laptop to transfer it over. It didn't happen. Bob in IT had thought the job would require less time. Got tied up. Forgot for a while.

Meanwhile, this morning I noticed that my diabetes meds would run out before I come back to work after Thanksgiving, and today would be my last day to get a refill. I called my pharmacy and learned they could have it ready before they closed at five o'clock.

I had hoped to get my new laptop by four o'clock so I could stop by the pharmacy before they closed.

At 4:15 when I went down to the IT office, Bob said he could have James finish the transfer job. So I ran to the pharmacy, and my meds were ready.

I got back after five o'clock and raced to IT. Bob was gone. James apologized that the laptop transfer wasn't done. I had more stuff on it than Bob had thought. I could either have my new laptop with only some files on it, or have my old laptop back and we could try the transfer again after Thanksgiving.

So I have my old laptop back—the one I've wanted to get rid of for years. It came defective, and it has just sort of held together with all of its quirks. Sometimes we get lucky, and sometimes we don't. And there are worse things than having to use this laptop for two more weeks. But I had my hopes up. And was disappointed.

As I stood in line at the pharmacy, I watched someone get upset that their meds weren't ready. When the pharmacist tried to explain to the man that he'd called in one prescription but not the other—and that they would take care of it right away—that didn't lessen the customer's anger. He glared for a while before sitting down.

We've all been the guy who forgot something or wasn't clear. And we've all had expectations that someone didn't live up to. Or discovered that something took more time than we expected.

And yet as I write this on my old laptop, I find myself asking what really matters here. The guy had to wait, but he got his medicine. I got my old laptop back and can continue to do the things I need to do. I got home at seven o'clock instead of six o'clock.

After I ate dinner, I caught up on some email and watched TV. I did some cleaning and enjoyed the quiet. It was the evening I'd hoped for after a long week.

I wonder about the guy who had to wait on his prescriptions. I wonder how he was doing this evening. I wonder if he's always been the way he was in the pharmacy. I wonder if he's been yelled at a lot himself. I wonder how the pharmacist did after being yelled at. And I wonder how Bob did after feeling bad about my computer.

We all let people down. We get side-tracked, busy. We all have been the recipient of other people's disappointment with us. And we've all been let down and disappointed by others.

Yet do we respond the same way when we're the ones who are disappointed and when we're the ones doing the disappointing? When we're disappointed, do we treat people the way we'd like to be treated when we're the ones who disappoint?

Maybe what really matters is that whatever we do or don't do, however we disappoint or not, there are more important things to focus on and bigger problems in the world. Maybe we'll be happier if we remember kindness in the face of the disappointments life brings.

I had dinner at a place with good reviews of their gluten-free pizza. I was seated at the bar and served by a woman who started right out apologizing that they didn't have lemons for the iced tea.

"I don't like lemon in my iced tea," I said.

She brightened. "That's the right answer," she said.

I ordered the gluten-free pizza with pepperoni, mushroom, and tomatoes. She thought that sounded delicious.

The reviews were not high enough. Best gluten-free pizza to date. I decided I might have to go back there before leaving town the following week.

The server's name was Wendy. She handed me the check when I had eaten the whole pizza, and said, "Whenever you're ready, but don't rush."

After I paid her, Wendy decided to be even more helpful. "Just be careful with the guys in the park," she said.

I'd seen two guys in wheelchairs. Clearly homeless. Lots of stuff around them, most of it under blankets.

"I'm glad I don't have their life," I said to Wendy. "I can't imagine what traumas they live with."

Wendy gave me a look.

I shrugged. "War vets?" I wondered out loud. "Maybe drugs and alcohol. Probably no support from family to help them cope. And all alone except other homeless guys. I bet they have some skills you and I might never have."

She just nodded and then said simply, "Thank you."

I smiled and left a larger than usual tip. I said hello to the two homeless guys and got in my car, but not before I looked back and saw Wendy at the restaurant window. She waved, and I waved back.

I hoped the nights would not be cold or wet over the coming months for the two guys in the park. And that made me think of all homeless people, and wonder whether things will ever get better for them. I also hoped Wendy would look out the restaurant window at the guys in wheelchairs through new, improved lenses.

Here is a tale of two realities during a pandemic.

First, glasses fixed—without ever going into the optician's shop. I handed them off from outside to the optician, who unlocked the door and stuck his_arm out. He looked at them after closing the door, opened it again a crack, and said, "Fairly easy. Should be about five minutes. You can wait here or in your car." Then he locked the door again and disappeared.

Six minutes later, he returned, unlocked the door, stuck his gloved hand out, and said, "Put them on and look in the glass for your reflection."

By the time I'd put my glasses on, he'd locked the door again. By the time I'd seen my reflection in the mirror, he was back inside, looking at me from a distance. When he caught my eye, he gave me a tentative thumbs up, which I returned.

Second, I stopped at the grocery store, where I did the anti-mating dance of a deranged roadrunner to avoid the crowds of people who seemed to have no issues with being in their own worlds and not thinking about social distancing. But I got some cheese and ham and sugar-free pudding and headed home.

To be fair, nearly everyone at the grocery store had on a mask. But I firmly believe the more we are careless about mingling, the longer we'll have to wait to be finished with this pandemic.

To today's store greeter: Yes, the cart may have been cleaned before the child crawled all over it, but afterwards it wasn't clean.

The mom decided to pick another cart because the one her child had attached itself to had clearly been in the rain.

As the mother selected another cart (while her child reluctantly detached), the greeter looked at me and said, "Take it. It's clean."

Quandary: Apparently neither the mother nor the greeter understood that social distancing is still an issue when it involves a child. Indeed the mother seemed oblivious of her child as she spent several lingering moments looking for the driest cart.

The greeter looked at me quizzically and then with annoyance.

I finally told him, "I'll just wait."

When the child had finally gotten off the cart, the greeter looked questioningly at me.

I just held up my hand. I was grateful no one had entered behind me who also wanted a cart. Fortunately, I saw the store's sanitary wipes put out for customers' use. I went and got one.

By the time I was back, the mother and child had left. The greeter just looked at me, frowning.

"I'm sure you cleaned it before the child touched it," I said. It took a second. Realization set in as I did a wipe-down. "And I couldn't take the cart and be more than six feet away from the child."

Another realization dawned across his face. "You should have said something."

"Well, I had time," I said. "And I feel for every parent right now. I figured a little patience would go a long way. Plus, being diabetic, I am a bit cautious."

I suppose I could have said something while the mother and her child were still there, and then both of them might have had a moment. But I had the time. And maybe at least the greeter will remember that, in the midst of a pandemic, the world is different now.

When I was driving this morning, suddenly there was a guy weaving recklessly by me. He made it to the stop light one car length ahead of me and some 15 seconds before I did—only to have to wait for the light to turn. I was afraid he was going to hit my car, but he didn't.

Yesterday, crossing the interstate on a foot bridge, I saw that the backed-up cars below me were standing still. Given that it was 11:00 in the morning, I was sure there had been accident. Even at rush hour, traffic moved faster than this.

I thought about the driver who had caused the accident that had surely happened, about everyone else involved in it, and about the fact that in an instant all those lives had changed because of it, perhaps forever. I don't know if that driver was reckless, but I do know that their day was now a whole lot different than planned.

But everyone's days are now different than planned. The driver who caused an accident no longer had control of their day. Today's reckless driver was trying to be more in control—and it made me wonder if he was always that way, or if he'd gotten worse during the pandemic. Was his car the one place out in the world where life felt normal to him and where he felt in control—at least somewhat—because he could speed and he could make a game or a contest out of driving, where he didn't have to change his preferred behavior? Where, at least as far as he knew, he still mattered more than others?

There's a term that entered our common vocabulary recently—"toxic individualism." I thought of that term today while I was thinking about the person who likely caused an accident yesterday and the one who nearly hit me today. The pandemic has brought out the best and the worst in all of us. It's easy to point fingers elsewhere (which perhaps is in itself a form of toxic individualism), but I suspect that during the past months we all have had moments when we put our own wants over what the world needs.

Our relationship to time is different now. We have both more and less of it. More time to think and feel. Less time to be in our own worlds, oblivious to all that is around us—though I think this morning's driver was doing his level best to win the Oblivious Olympics. I wonder what we'll learn from this pandemic. What new behaviors will become habitual? What old patterns will be forgotten? What accidents will cause us to stop and let go? What need for control will make us move faster?

I hope yesterday's driver is okay and living into a new day today having learned something, even if it's only to pay more attention to others nearby. I hope this morning's driver doesn't need an accident in order to change and prioritize life beyond the self. And finally I hope I have the self-awareness to notice when I'm behaving just like this morning's driver—speeding in a race that I have conjured up myself and weaving through life without paying attention to those around me. At such a moment, may I be able to slow down and focus on the road ahead, wherever it might take me.

Tonight when I went out for groceries, I chose the self-scan-and-pay line. I paid, asked for cash back, and headed out.

A moment later, the woman who monitors the eight registers was calling out, "Sir! Sir!" and waving my cash, which I'd forgotten to collect. She grabbed a sanitary wipe at the entrance where they have some out for people to use to clean their cart handles, wiped off my money, and then delicately handed it to me, while I profusely thanked her.

She waved off my thanks. "You're the fourth person tonight to do that. People have a lot on their minds during this pandemic," she said with a smile, and then waved me off.

The challenge for all of us is to be that kind and caring every day.

It was good to see Jeanne, even briefly, at the store again after we've been essentially in lock-down for months during the pandemic. She was bagging groceries while I was down a few aisles at the self-service checkout. She gave a hearty wave, and I could see her eyes light up when I waved back. I stopped by when I was done and asked how she'd been doing.

"Oh, I'm as ornery as ever." She laughed.

"Thank you for your consistency and dependability," I deadpanned back to her, and then broke into a grin as we chuckled together.

"It's the least I can do." She grinned and then went on, "It's been a while since I've seen you."

"Well, we're finally playing tennis again, and you all are open past eight o'clock now. So I have a bit of time to stop in."

"Yes, they had me on the morning shift," she said, "and I'm not a morning person. So it's good to be back closer to my normal schedule. I'm more of a vampire than anything."

"Well, I've heard vampires are ornery. Thanks for the confirmation." I headed off with a wave and light, infectious laughter coming from behind me. It's really the little things that make for a good day. And it's been a good day.

Epilogue

December 15, 2020

Dear Cynthia,

I was out on my morning walk today, and I saw a feral cat across the street. He stopped and looked at me. He reminded me a bit of your Elvis and I said out loud to him, and perhaps to you as well, "But can you juggle pit bulls?" The cat sped off at that remark, which was hardly a surprise. It didn't matter. I chuckled aloud, a wry grin of memory spreading across my face. That did matter.

The world has changed a lot since you left. Walking the streets of my neighborhood 10 days before Christmas, I still see election signs along with the holiday decorations and lights, and lots of bags of leaves. There are also lots of Black Lives Matter signs, which are new this year and a welcome addition to the scene. I get a lot of looks from plaintive dogs who don't understand the pandemic and really don't understand why I won't come over and pet them and say hello. The December sun is weaker now but still warms me. It lifts my spirits to be out in the world. I take everything in, pleased to be witnessing it all.

I wish you were here to see all this, knowing you too would have witnessed and loved all of it. Maybe you are here after all—reminding me to pay attention, to notice, to celebrate.

Your death was supposed to hurt. Grief is a normal companion. I lost a kindred spirit when you died but what you taught me, I have carried forward. The world around me has taught me in a deeper way that life with a weaker sun is still life, still worth celebrating. You taught me that grief also becomes a reminder of how fortunate I was to have been connected so deeply to another person.

Cynthia, thank you for the grief. I am constantly reminded I am not alone, even when it seems that way. Your stories and your life live on within me. Our friendship taught me to be present and to revel in the wild and wonderful ways of life around me. The sun will continue to warm. The world will continue to change. The stories that abound will continue to matter. I don't know if I'll learn to juggle all of them before I find cats that can manage three pit bulls in the air, but I'll keep trying.

Thank you for being such a great companion. I'll keep witnessing life. I'll keep writing. Jack, Elvis, and I still miss you.

Love, Keith

Acknowledgements

This book would not have been possible without the efforts of certain people.

A huge thanks to all those who have encouraged this into being. My cousin Beverly Stooksbury Leitner, who is funnier than I am and who always makes me laugh. My former teaching colleague Diane Larricchia Benezet, who shares my love of reading, perspective, and storytelling. Both were insistent this happen.

Thanks to my parents, Ken and Kathy Kron, my sister Karen Hamilton, and her two children Richard and Shay Hamilton for always being there. To my cousins, Terri, Ken, David, Joan, Lisa, Sherri, and their families, who ground me in my Appalachian roots.

Thanks to my ministerial colleagues, especially all who knew Cynthia, who were so supportive when Cynthia died.

Thanks to all the students I taught (who are now all adults). They taught me so many things, including how much a story could make a difference. My thanks to them for listening—at least sometimes.

Thanks to co-workers and colleagues at the Unitarian Universalist Association: Jory Agate, Tracy Barry, Sofia Betancourt, Taquiena Boston, Emily Cherry, Patrice Curtis, Danielle diBona, Robette Dias, Alicia Forde, Jan Gartner, Devorah Greenstein, Barb Greve, Mel Hoover, John Hurley, Jacqui James, Hope Johnson, Janice Marie Johnson, Paula Cole Jones, Sarah Lammert, Susan Leslie, Diane Martin, Jean McKenney, Margaret Montore, Simona Munseeney, Richard Nugent, Christine Purcell, Meg Riley, Tracey Robinson-Harris, Linda Rose, Julie Shaw, Bill Sinkford, Leon Spencer, and Marta Valentin. Whether it is for teaching me about anti-racism and anti-oppression, or simply for supporting our joint work, I give my profound and forever thanks.

To my chosen family, Kris, Shirley, Casey, Beatrice, Jim, Elizabeth, Wayne, JoAnna, Portia, Jessica, and Chris, thanks for being there—even when distance gets in the way. To my tennis family, thanks for the balance and lobbing short. To my friends, wherever they are, thanks for making my life better and these stories possible.

My biggest thank you is to my dear friend and colleague, Rev. Barbara Child. Her passion, vigilance, and hard work have made this book possible. This truly would not have happened without her. I am forever grateful.

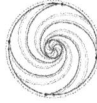

About the Author

For the past decade, Rev. Keith Kron has been the Director of the Transitions Office for the Unitarian Universalist Association (UUA), helping congregations and ministers as they navigate the ministerial search process. For the previous decade and a half, he was the UUA's Director of the Office of Bisexual, Gay, Lesbian, and Transgender Concerns.

During his 25 years of service to the UUA, Kron has visited over 450 Unitarian Universalist congregations, from Fairbanks, Alaska, to Fort Lauderdale, Florida, and from Honolulu, Hawaii, to St. John's, Newfoundland. He has authored congregational training materials including *Living the Welcoming Congregation* and written a premarital counseling guide for same-sex couples. He coordinates the UUA's Beyond Categorical Thinking program, which promotes non-discrimination in ministerial search. He also leads anti-racism trainings for the UUA and has co-chaired the UUA's Family Matters Task Force. He has worked with congregations witnessing for marriage equality and has supported congregations in difficult times of conflict and harassment.

Kron's Master of Divinity degree is from Starr King School for the Ministry, a Unitarian Universalist seminary. Before becoming a minister, he was an active lay leader. He served as chair of the UUA's General Assembly Planning Committee. He chaired Interweave Continental, an organization of congregation-based groups that worked to end oppression based on sexual orientation and gender identity. He served as president of the Midwest Unitarian Universalist Summer Assembly. He served on his home district's board for five years and his home congregation's board for seven years. While still a layperson, he won a UUA Annual Program Fund award for best sermon on giving and money.

Before becoming a minister, Kron was an elementary school teacher, a football and basketball referee, a softball umpire, and painter of school gymnasiums and parking lots.

He has co-authored a children's book, *About Right and Wrong*. He was a contributor of resources on good children's literature to the UUA's church without walls called the Church of the Larger Fellowship. As a minister, he has been an adjunct professor of religious education for Starr King School for the Ministry and has taught an online course for the school on children's literature. He has created a special Harry Potter Jeopardy game and is considered by many an expert on Harry Potter. His personal collection of children's books numbers over 9,000.

Kron's publications also include: *Coming Out in Faith* (co-editor), *In the Interim* (co-editor), *The Abundance of Our Faith* (author of a chapter titled "Theology of Money and Fair Exchange"), and *Defending Same Sex Marriage* (author of a chapter titled "Unitarian Universalism and Same Sex Marriage"). He served for 10 years on the Board of Directors of Skinner House Books.

In his spare time, Kron enjoys playing and teaching tennis, working out, cycling, reading, and leading trainings on the Enneagram. He also haunts bookstores.

9 780578 887098